TOKYO
City Guide

IBC Publishing

Cover design by Stone Bridge Press.
Cover photos by Aflo.

Introduction

I once heard if you want to write a travel book about a place, you need to do it within the first three months after your arrival. Otherwise, the uncommon will begin to seem common and you'll lose the perspective you need to write from the viewpoint of a tourist.

I've lived in Tokyo for almost 25 years now, but perhaps the reason I feel I am still qualified to write a book for tourists is because of the enormous size and great diversity of Tokyo. After all my years here, I still feel like a tourist, and almost every time I go out, I feel like I'm going on a little trip to make new discoveries.

This desire to continue exploring Tokyo is often augmented when I talk to someone who's been here for a shorter period of time than I have, sometimes only a few days, but still knows something about Tokyo that I've never heard about! While I think I know the basics of Tokyo, Tokyo is constantly changing in many ways, so there's always something new in this old city.

This book focuses on the parts of Tokyo that I think will be around for several years to come, so hopefully the information presented here will be accurate and helpful for a long time. As for the newer parts of Tokyo, the parts that even I haven't discovered yet, I hope you are able to experience them once you come to Tokyo.

Perhaps one of the most important discoveries you will make during your visit is how helpful Japanese people are. Japanese are generally very interested in making sure you have a great time in Japan and leave with a good impression of their country. While there are exceptions, you'll find that asking for directions or other information is a great icebreaker, and most Japanese will do all they can to help.

Welcome to Japan!
David Thayne

Contents

Introduction 3

Chapter 1
The Basics 7

Getting around *9*
Where to stay *16*
Eating *22*
Japanese etiquette *30*
Money and shopping *36*
When in trouble *42*

Chapter 2
The Seasons 45

Winter *47*
Spring and rainy season *54*
Summer *60*
Autumn *66*

Chapter 3
The Places.................................. 73

Asakusa Area *75*
Ueno Area *80*
Tokyo Station Area *86*
Shibuya Area *96*
Shinjuku Area *102*
Akasaka / Roppongi / Azabu Area *108*
Odaiba Area *114*
Musashino Area *122*
Kamakura Area *128*

Appendix.................................. *141*

Everything else *143*
Holidays in Japan *149*
Who to call *153*

Index *154*

The Basics

Getting around

Tokyo has taxis, buses and rental cars, but for people who think about convenience and cost, trains are the best way to go.

Japanese trains are very punctual, and even if they are a few minutes late, there is an announcement which apologizes and explains the reason for the delay. If there is an LCD screen inside of the train, the name of the next station will be shown on it, just in case you weren't able to catch the Japanese announcement.

If you avoid the peak morning and evening rush hours, you might not get a seat, but you won't find yourself cheek to cheek with a stranger either.

• Trains

Tokyo is known for having one of the best train systems in the world, but they can also be among the most packed. Just remember that no matter where you are in Tokyo, you can probably find a train station within walking distance. Tokyo train lines are a mixture of both public lines, known as JR (for Japan Railways) and various private train companies, as well as a network of subway lines connected to most major train stations. Normally, you can count on a train arriving and leaving exactly at its scheduled time. This means a train arriving even two minutes later may be the wrong one! You can find maps of the train lines in English at tourist centers, major hotels and online, and some station workers can usually direct you to the right trains in simple English.

Now, a warning about the rush hours: major train lines in the morning and evening commuting hours can be so congested that sometimes railroad staff have to push people onto the train so that the doors can shut. If possible, you'll want to avoid those hours, unless you want to experience being packed into a train like a sardine!

- **Taxis**

Just as trains make traveling in Tokyo convenient, the huge number of taxis in Tokyo

Taxis can be a little expensive, but they're comfortable and safe. *Kure*

also makes it easy to go wherever the train won't take you at any hour of the day or night. At any major train station or hotel, there will probably be several different taxi companies just waiting for passengers, so you won't even need to telephone for one.

There are a couple of things you should know about riding in a Japanese taxi, however. First, you don't need to open the door yourself. The driver will open it and close it automatically for you—but that's only if you enter on the left side, the passenger side.

Second, the driver will probably understand you if you state clearly where you want to go, though you'll encounter cab drivers with varying English proficiency.

The third, and best thing, is that you don't need to tip the driver. The driver will generally give you back your exact change, but when I come across a friendly and helpful driver (and many are), I will let the driver keep the small change, say 100 or 200 yen, as a sign of thanks.

• **Local buses, Bus tours**

Metropolitan buses are a convenient way to travel to places not well served by trains, or when you're too tired to walk. The only drawback is the routes can be very confusing if you don't know exactly where you're going. Also, depending on the bus, it can be difficult to find information or destination names in English.

Public buses within the 23 Wards is 210 yen for all passengers over 12 (August, 2014). You need to board from the door near the driver and put the money in a little box. When you want to get off, push the button near your seat to let the driver know. Exit from the rear door.

If you're in a sightseeing mood, a popular bus service for foreigners is the Hato Bus tours. These tourist buses offer half-day or full-day tours of Tokyo's popular tourist sites, complete with guides for major languages. Information about the many tours offered can be found online.

A Hato Bus tour is great way to see Tokyo in a few hours.

• Bicycles

Bicycle rental shops are available around many tourist destinations in Tokyo, often found at train stations. Rental bicycles can be an alternative means of transportation when it is too far to go to a certain location on foot, and can be more convenient than buses and less expensive than taxis for short distances.

The most common type of bicycle at a rental shop, called a *mamachari* in Japanese, is a simple bicycle for everyday use. They usually come equipped with a front basket, light, bell, lock and one gear, but this is usually enough to get you to your destination. When renting a bicycle, be ready to pay a deposit and have a photo ID and your accommodation details (address and phone number) on hand, just in case they request it. Rental fees can be from as low as 100 yen per hour and up to about 1,000 yen for a whole day.

In Japan, you normally would ride on the streets or roads and not the sidewalk, unless there are signs indicating that the sidewalk is usable by both pedestrians and cyclists. However, many locals and cyclists often don't follow this rule nor is it enforced by the authorities. Wearing a helmet is optional, and rental shops usually don't provide them.

Do's and don'ts of travel

✔ On long-distance trains, go ahead and bring food to enjoy. In fact, stations or the trains will sell *bentos* (lunch-boxes) for train passengers to eat while they ride.

A special type of boxed lunch sold on train stations.

✔ If you have to get on an extremely crowded train, stay close to the exit if you have to get off soon. Otherwise, you might not be able to get out at your stop.

✔ On buses, you should try to have your fare ready to avoid holding up other passengers, but if you need change, there will also be a machine to change money where you deposit your fare.

✔ When riding a bicycle on the road, stay to the far left side following the same direction as traffic (people drive on the left in Japan). In Japan, it is illegal to ring your bicycle bell. However, it's okay to use it if you're in danger. That being said, the proper etiquette is to get off of your bike and walk or give the person in front of you a verbal warning.

- ✔ Don't eat food on inner-city commuter trains.

- ✔ Don't sit in the seats marked for handicapped people, pregnant women or senior citizens, unless a train or bus has plenty of open seats.

- ✔ If you're a male, make sure you don't get on a train car reserved for women. Many trains in Tokyo have such special cars so women can ride safely. Women only train cars run in the mornings and at night.

A sign on a subway car window.

- ✔ If you can't find a seat on a train, don't sit on the floor! You may see some young people doing that, but it's bad manners and also prohibited.

- ✔ Don't talk on your cell-phone on trains and buses. That is also prohibited.

- ✔ Don't park your bicycle in any random area, especially at places with signs that clearly say not to, as this is prohibited. If you do, your bicycle may be removed by the authorities, after which you would have to pay a fine to get it back. Instead, use the designated parking areas usually found around train stations or in front of attractions.

Getting around

Where to stay

One thing that may shock you and your pocketbook about staying in Japan is that a lot of hotels charge by the person and not the room. So make sure you're clear about that when making reservations. But regardless of the cost, most hotels in Japan provide friendly service. The ones that cater to foreign visitors will have a lot of information in English, but most hotels will do their best to make your stay comfortable.

• High-end inns and hotels

Tokyo has some of the world's fanciest and most expensive hotels, and if you can afford it, you'll have the chance to stay in luxurious surroundings and receive superb service from extremely polite staff. Many of the high-end hotels, including international hotel chains, have free shuttle bus service from Narita or Haneda airport as well. A more traditional place to stay is a Japanese inn called a *ryokan*, often located in more scenic areas. At a *ryokan*, you may sleep on a futon, on a Japanese *tatami* floor, and you may likely be served a luxurious, traditional dinner within your own room. A *ryokan* will also have a spacious bath, sometimes an *onsen* to share with other guests, and sometimes your own private bath.

A typical high-end hotel in Yokohama area.

To find a traditional hotel in Japan, visit this site:
http://Japantraveleronline.com

Where to stay

• Low-end inns and hotels

Like all major cities in the world, Tokyo also has youth hostels that serve adventurous international travelers, easily found online. But Tokyo also has a variety of inexpensive hotels and inns that offer an interesting experience to foreign travelers. One of the most common, and perhaps least unique, is a simple "business hotel," usually located in the neighborhood of major train stations. The cost for one night is usually under 10,000 yen, and in return you get a clean but very small room, typically for one or two people, with a combined bath/shower and toilet.

A more traditional Japanese inn, called a *minshuku*, can be found in metropolitan Tokyo, but they're more common in rural areas or small cities. You might think of a *minshuku* as a Japanese version of a bed-and-breakfast, indeed, sometimes in someone's private home.

In many cases, you're expected to bring your own towel and toiletries, or those may be available for a small price. And you may also end up sharing the inn's public bath with other guests.

Probably the most unique lodging experience you can find is in a "capsule hotel," literally just that: you will sleep in a small capsule, situated on top of the capsule of another guest. Inside your "capsule" you may have a TV or stereo, but the bath facilities are all public.

Check the websites below to find interesting places to stay in your price range.

www.j-hostel.com/usabashi/?language=en

www.sakura-hostel.co.jp/

www.libertyhouse.gr.jp/

http://www.tokyoryokan.com/

Do's and don'ts of hotels

✔ If you stay at a traditional Japanese inn, either a low-end *minshuku* or a high-end *ryokan*, you can feel free to walk around the hotel wearing the *yukata* provided to you. A *yukata* is the thin, full-length bathrobe (that many foreigners mistake for being a kimono). *Yukatas* are provided so you can feel relaxed, inside or outside your room, and you'll likely see other guests walking around in theirs.

The *yukata* makes a great bathrobe.

✔ Do make sure you know the lobby closing hours—you might not be able to get in if you return late in the evening.

✔ Do be aware that many hotels have certain places where you can and can't wear shoes. If you need to take off your shoes, it will usually be clearly marked.

✔ If you'd like a wake-up call, you will be clearly understood if you ask for a "morning call."

✔ Do ask questions at the front desk. They're one of the best sources for information about restaurants and nearby activities.

✔ When a bellhop type of person helps carry your bags to your room, don't tip him or her —it's not expected.

✔ Don't think the hotel staff is talking about a religious service if they tell you about "morning service." They're probably talking about the breakfast that goes with the room.

✔ When staying at a Japanese style hotel, don't be surprised if the room maid suddenly comes into your room to serve tea or food, or to remove your futon from the closet.

✔ Don't leave a bed-making tip, but do show your respect by straightening up the room.

✔ At any of the hotels, even the international hotel chains, once again, you don't need to worry about tipping, be it the baggage staff who brings your bags to your room, or the maids, when you stay multiple days. However, if you feel like leaving a small gratuity at the end of your stay, it's not frowned upon in hotels.

Eating

Tokyo has the most Michelin starred restaurants worldwide of any city. Some restaurants are very expensive, including Aragawa, a Kobe-beef steakhouse that will cost you at least 35,000 yen per person.

But if that's a little over your budget, you'll be glad to know that Japan has a lot of wonderful places to eat for even 500 yen or less.

• Menus

The most difficult thing you may find about a Japanese menu is that, well, it's in Japanese. Restaurants that foreign customers often eat at, as well as many fast-food restaurant chains, may have an English copy of the menu if you need it. But many restaurants, especially restaurant chains known as "family restaurants" will have pictures of the food items, so if you don't read Japanese, you only have to point to the picture. And you'll discover that most restaurants in department stores, shopping malls, or even on the street will also have a display window in front, with delicious-looking wax sculptures of most or all of the menu items. If you end up with a menu you can't understand, you can simply point to the food you want in the display window!

• **Price and tipping**

The nice thing about the cost of eating in Tokyo is that what you see is what you get! The price on the menu will normally include the tax, and tipping is absolutely not necessary in Japan. You never need to worry about leaving your waiter a tip. It's still uncommon in Japan to pay your bill at the table; more likely, you'll need to take your bill to a cashier near the exit of the restaurant, and pay there. At more casual restaurants or cafeterias, however, you may be required to buy a meal ticket before you sit down. If you're in doubt, the restaurant staff will probably help you.

• **Breakfast**

While you may find some 24-hour restaurant chains, you might be surprised how hard it is to find a restaurant open for breakfast, but a good place to start are at restaurants known in Japanese as *kissaten*, or coffee shops. Such coffee shops can be found near most stations in the metropolitan area, and they are known for their "morning set" or "morning service" (pronounced *mohningu setto* and *mohningu saabisu*), typically serving eggs (fried, scrambled or boiled), a piece of toast with jam, salad and coffee or orange juice. Otherwise, you can generally find breakfast served at most fast-food chains.

You'll also find Japanese eating breakfast at specialty restaurants that you might not associate with breakfast, such as those serving curry and rice or beef and rice bowls. But then, many foreigners may be surprised to see salad as a typical breakfast dish in Japan!

• **Lunch**

Possibly the biggest challenge you'll face in finding a place to eat lunch in Tokyo is finding one that is not crowded. During the lunch hours between 11 a.m. and 1 p.m., many restaurants are crowded on the weekdays with workers on their lunch-breaks, and on the weekends with shoppers.

At popular restaurants, you might typically have to wait 20 to 30 minutes for a table. Fast-food restaurants can serve you more quickly, but they still may be more crowded than what you're used to. To avoid such crowds, I find it easier to adjust my eating times, eating a little earlier or later than the normal lunch crowd.

But large restaurants aren't your only option for lunch. You'll probably witness a lot of office workers grabbing a quick lunch at a *ramen* or *soba* noodle stand, sometimes even on the platform of a train station. Or you might see Japanese on a park bench eating a *bento*, or boxed lunch, from a nearby convenience store.

• Dinner

Unless you're planning a large-scale dinner party, or attempting to eat at famous sushi restaurants that have limited seating, it's unlikely you'll need to make a reservation for dinner at most restaurants you'd visit during a stay in Tokyo. Tokyo is known for its gourmet cuisine, and you can find a restaurant that will serve just about any type of food you can imagine, including all types of international foods.

If you're seeking a more "local" experience might look for a *yakitori* restaurant, which is an often cozy, casual restaurant where you can get all types of grilled meat and vegetables served on a skewer (although the word *yakitori* itself refers to grilled chicken), with various side dishes and drinks also available.

A popular type of restaurant among Japanese is the *kaiten-zushi* restaurant, where small plates of various kinds of sushi revolve on a conveyer belt in front of customers, who pick what they want and pay based on the number of dishes consumed. These plates are usually color coded with each color costing a different amount. There should be a key located on the wall of the restaurant or somewhere around where you are seated. These days, *kaiten-zushi* restaurants offer many things other than sushi. There are some stores that even have French fries, *ramen*, parfaits and coffee!

• **Street food**

Wherever there's a festival going on, you'll be sure to find street vendors.

Takoyaki, balls of cooked batter with octopus meat inside, is perhaps the most common street food and the easiest to come across.

Another common food sold by vendors or in stalls is *yakitori*, or grilled chicken on a skewer.

There are also many vendors selling *okonomiyaki*, sometimes called a Japanese pancake, which is made with pork or seafood with vegetables, cooked in a pancake-like batter and coated in special sauces and Japanese mayonnaise.

You can also find Western treats such as corn dogs, called *American dogs*, French fries, called *fried potato*, and crepes.

• **Vegetarians**

If you eat fish, you'll have no trouble finding something to eat, but if you don't, it can be quite difficult since a lot of meat-free dishes are made with a soup stock made from bonito.

There are many pure vegetarian and vegan restaurants, but you'll need to do some searching on the Internet, at perhaps HappyCow.net, to find them.

One possibility is to go to a conveyor-belt sushi restaurant where you can see what you're getting before you pick it up off the conveyor belt, and there are surprising many items that don't have fish.

Japanese love Indian food, so it's not hard to find an Indian restaurant that understands the vegetarian's heart and stomach.

Convenience stores and grocery shops have a lot of nice deli foods, so you can see what you're getting before you get it, and then you can enjoy eating it in a nearby park—good way to save money.

Do's and don'ts of eating

✔ Despite what you might have read elsewhere, slurping your food is NOT a sign that the food is delicious and NOT a compliment to the cook. You can slurp two things—hot noodles (you'll burn your mouth if you don't) and cold noodles (you'll need to slurp up the sauce to make the noodles more tasty). Making a lot of noise when eating other types of food is a sign that you have poor manners.

✔ Don't worry about being served raw horse or chicken. Raw fish in Japan is common, raw horse is almost never heard of, and raw chicken is almost never ever heard of. If you look really hard you can find a few places in Tokyo that serve raw meat, but most Japanese find the thought of eating any type of flesh besides fish unthinkable.

✔ If you're in a crowded restaurant at lunch time, don't spend too much time occupying your table chatting, reading or relaxing after you've finished. There are likely people waiting for a table, and the restaurant would like to serve as many people as possible.

✔ Proper etiquette at a traditional Japanese restaurant can be very complicated—even for Japanese. But Japanese are very forgiving of foreigners—especially if you make a good effort to follow the customs and are pleasant.

✔ Don't expect the waiter to come to your table when you are ready to pay your bill. In most cases, you'll pay at the cash register.

✔ At a local-type of restaurant, don't be surprised if you're seated next to a stranger. It's very common in this crowded country.

✔ Don't be too confused by the vending machines at the entrance to a lot of cheaper restaurants. To save costs, you need to buy a ticket at the door. Many fast-food restaurants will have pictures of the food and their prices on these ticket vending machines, so you can easily find most items on the menu. The change is not usually paid out automatically, so you'll need to push a lever of some type to get your change back. Then take the slip of paper from the vending machine to the counter or table and show the server.

✔ Do try out the Japanese pastries. Japanese are very particular about the food they eat, but the pastries lovers can be particularly fickle, resulting in some of the most amazing desserts in the world, if you ask me.

Japanese etiquette

One thing Japan is famous for is complicated etiquette—it's definitely true. Luckily for non-Japanese visitors, Japanese are very tolerant, especially if you're patient and friendly. Partly just to be nice and partly for the cultural experience, I would try to follow Japanese etiquette, but there are actually very few things you can accidently do to insult or anger Japanese.

• Bowing

A commonly held stereotype of Japanese people is that they always bow. Like many stereotypes, however, there is some truth to it. When exchanging business cards (very common and almost a must in Japan), people will bow slightly as they offer their card with both hands. Many Japanese who have regular contact with foreigners won't hesitate to offer a handshake, but don't expect to find anyone who gives a kiss on the cheek! You may be surprised to see sales staff of upscale department stores or hotels standing at the entrance offering deep bows to customers.

• Taking off your shoes

In general, expect to take off your shoes whenever you enter a Japanese home. Wearing shoes inside a home is considered unsanitary in Japan, and all houses, condominiums and apartments have an entrance area called a *genkan* where guests can take off and leave their shoes.

If you are a guest, your hosts may put out slippers for you to wear around the house. However, if you enter a room with *tatami* mats (made of woven rice straw), you must remove these slippers beforehand. There are also separate slippers for bathrooms, which you are expected to change into upon entering the bathroom.

Most western-style hotels allow you to wear shoes inside your room, but Japanese-style inns or restaurants may have you remove your shoes. If you see a *genkan* and *tatami* floors in front of you, you can be sure shoes are not allowed.

• Visiting someone's home

Besides removing your shoes, if you're visiting someone's home, it's commonly expected that you'll bring a small gift, typically some kind of gift-wrapped food or snack. A typical gift food item is *senbei*, or Japanese rice crackers. Your Japanese host will surely observe traditional manners by serving you a cup of green tea and a small dessert or snack. Modern Japanese homes may have chairs for you to sit on, but many homes still have a traditional *tatami* room for guests, where you will sit on the floor around a low table.

• **Trains**

If you're on the train, refrain from talking on your phone or talking loudly in general. I picked this up after a few trips on the train. You don't want to get dirty looks from other passengers. If you want to read a newspaper on the train, try to keep it folded so it doesn't invade your neighbor's personal space. Doing your makeup on the train is also frowned upon. The same generally goes for eating, but eating a small snack from your bag or pocket should be fine. Drinking fluids from resealable containers like plastic bottles is best, and refrain from drinking alcohol on the train. You may see others doing it, but they are technically breaking the rules.

• Hot springs (onsen)

Japanese are very sensitive to hot springs manners violations, so please be careful. The most important rule to observe is that you never enter the public bath without thoroughly washing yourself first. This can be done at a small shower or faucet located around the main bath. Body soap, shampoo and conditioner are usually available for you to use. Remember, you must never wash yourself in the bathtub itself.

The towel you use to wash yourself should also stay out of the bath water, but you may use it to cover your private parts as you walk around. One taboo that still remains in Japanese *onsen* are tattoos. While more and more young Japanese may have tattoos, *onsens* still frown upon them. If you have one, you can try covering it with a bandage, but they may still refuse to let you in. There are *onsens* that don't mind tattoos, however, sometimes even far off in the countryside. You might want to double check online before going.

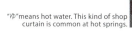

"ゆ" means hot water. This kind of shop curtain is common at hot springs.

Do's and don'ts of Japanese etiquette

✔ Go and ahead and try sitting Japanese-style on the floor (called *seiza*, with your legs folded underneath your behind), but don't hesitate to unfold your legs if it starts to become painful (and if you're not used to it, it will become painful).

✔ As a guest at someone's home, you might be treated to a traditional Japanese tea ceremony, where you are served a thick, bitter tea called *matcha*. There are special manners for drinking *matcha* in these cases, which you can feel free to ask your host about.

✔ If you bow to a Japanese person, don't hold your hands in front of you like you would in India when greeting somebody with the word "namaste." That is not a common Japanese gesture, and can be considered offensive.

✔ If you receive a business card from someone, don't casually stuff it into your pocket. Instead, carefully place it in your wallet or a name card holder, if you have one. If you are sitting at a table, place it on the table in front of you and leave it there as you continue to speak with the person who gave it to you. You can put it away after a short while.

✔ While there are some big exceptions, most Japanese are quiet-spoken in public. It's generally considered best to keep your voice down when in crowds.

✔ Do consider your body language. Japanese body language is usually more subdued than Western body language. Crossing your legs, folding your arms and standing with your hands on your waist might make you look more aloof and cold than your intent.

✔ You probably know that Japanese don't wear shoes in the house, but you might also be asked to remove them when entering a temple or shrine building. Having holes in your socks is one of the easiest ways to lose face in Japan.

Money and shopping

As in every culture, Japan has some interesting customs from bygone days that survive as common sense. Due case in point is money. You'll find that Japanese bills are usually very clean and usually unfolded. If Japanese see money on the ground, they are probably less likely to pick it up than in most other cultures. And—to the surprise of many—the wife usually has full responsibility of how the money is spent in a household.

• Converting money

If you have foreign currency you need to exchange for yen, you can do it at most major banks which you'll find near most train stations within the city limits. But be careful: while you can usually easily exchange U.S. dollars or euros, and in the biggest banks, Korean *won* or Chinese *gen*, other foreign currencies are almost impossible to exchange once you leave the airport, so I would recommend exchanging your money at the airport. For withdrawing money from your bank account, ATMs at the 7-11 convenience store chains and some others accept most if not all international debit and credit cards and don't charge a high fee.

• Cash vs credit cards

One thing that may surprise you about shopping in or visiting Japan is that cash is still very much the norm, unlike many countries where cash is almost a thing of the past. Many Japanese don't hesitate to walk around with large amounts of cash in their wallets. In fact, there are times when it's almost impossible to use anything but cash.

Of course credit cards are used in many places as well (especially popular are cash cards which are similar to debit cards), but foreign visitors to Japan are often surprised to find that their international credit cards issued abroad aren't accepted in many stores or restaurants. That's why it's always nice to have some cash on hand just in case. There are also stores and restaurants that simply do not take anything but cash.

• Bills and coins

Besides coins for 1, 5, 10, 50, 100 and 500 yen, Japanese currency includes paper bills for 1,000, 5,000 and 10,000 yen. A 10,000 yen bill may seem like a lot when you convert it mentally to your country's currency, but in Japan it's common to carry such bills, and you can use them freely wherever you shop. In fact, most train ticket vending machines will accept such a large bill, although for other vending machines, such as for soft drinks, the largest bill you can use is 1,000 yen.

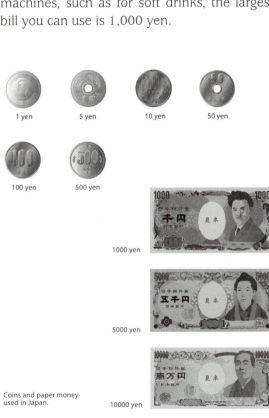

Coins and paper money used in Japan.

• Shopping

Tokyo is a wonderful city for shopping, although you might find the prices to be a little high. In Tokyo's major business areas, such as Ginza, Shinjuku and Shibuya, you can find large-scale department stores with everything in one huge building. Many tourists like to head to Akihabara, famous for its electronic and high-tech goods. But around most any station, large or small, you can find dozens of large and small shops selling anything from clothing to cameras. Don't overlook the 100-yen stores scattered around the city where you can get unique Japanese souvenirs for around 100 yen.

Tokyo is shopper's paradise!

Do's and don'ts of money

✔ In big department stores, do find time to visit the delicatessen/food floor (usually the first or second underground floor, called B1 and B2). You can usually find free samples of many delicious foods, and it's also a good place for buying souvenir food items.

✔ While bartering is common in some parts of Japan, it's not so common in Tokyo. You might ask once for a "small discount," but don't push too hard for a big discount.

✔ When a clerk bows to you, you don't need to bow back. But a simple "thank you" or *arigato*—or just a smile and a nod of the head—would be nice in return.

✔ Don't think you can spend U.S. dollars or any other currency. Very few stores allow this.

✔ Do make sure you can use your credit card before you decide what you're going to buy.

- ✔ Don't be surprised if tax gets added to your bill. The sales tax is usually included in the price, but not always.

- ✔ Don't worry too much about getting incorrect change. I'm not saying it doesn't happen, but my many years of shopping in Japan, it has only happened once or twice to me.

When in trouble

Very few Japanese people will ignore you if you ask them for help. If the person you ask for instructions can't help you, they'll usually find someone nearby for you who can. If you smile and say "Thank you," you'll have a good experience, and so will the Japanese person who helps you.

• When you're lost

In a city as huge and complicated as Tokyo, the chance that you might get lost shouldn't come as a surprise. If that happens, above all, don't panic. Tokyo may be huge, but it's still one of the world's safest cities, and most people will try to help you, so your first step might be just to ask the first person you can find. If you can locate a *koban*, or police box (mentioned below), don't hesitate to ask officers there. They'll pull out their large maps and show you the way.

• Police and police boxes

Tokyo police try to be helpful to everyone and are happy to help you if you're lost. And the police boxes are easy to locate. They're called *koban* in Japanese, and that word will be on the building in the Roman alphabet:

This symbol identifies police boxes located throughout Tokyo.

KOBAN. *Koban* are usually located in front of or near train stations, and even if the officers on duty don't speak much English, they'll do their best to help.

• When sick

Japan does not have a lot of imported medicines that you might be familiar with, but they do have alternatives. You'll need to go to a drugstore before they close in the evening, instead of a 24-hour convenience store, which are allowed to sell only limited kinds of medicine.

• When you need medical care

Japan does have excellent hospitals, and usually staff who speak English. Your embassy in Japan can usually offer specific information depending on your situation. It's a good idea to keep your embassy's emergency number on hand.

• When an earthquake hits

Japan has about 1,500 earthquakes each year, but of course most of them go unnoticed. From what we've seen in the past, Japanese tend to remain calm during serious earthquakes. The best advice I have for you is to basically do what the Japanese are around you. They are probably following the instructions from people in the know. Once every few years, an earthquake is strong enough to stop all trains, and so you might have to walk back to your hotel. I feel sorry for women who have to do it in high heels.

The Seasons

2

Winter

From late November to late January, it can get so cold that you might need to wear a coat, hat and gloves to keep warm. The average temperature in February ranges from 1 degree to 10 degrees Celsius, but it can feel much colder because of the wind chill from ocean gales and also strong winds created by buildings. On occasion, it even drops below zero. It is also not uncommon to see snow several times a year.

• Tori-no-ichi festival

Dates: the last weekend of November

One of the most well-known winter festivals is called Tori-no-ichi and takes place at temples and shrines throughout Tokyo on the last weekend of November. This event signals the arrival of winter and one of its trademarks is the *kumade* (an elaborately decorated ornamental bamboo rake), which you can find on sale at stalls all around the temple or shrine. The

The Festival of the Rooster.
Shu takinami

rakes are said to help "rake in" good fortune and prosperity. These rakes vary from small and simple designs to huge and elaborately decorated ones. If you ask at your hotel, they'll probably be able to direct you to such a festival going on nearby.

- **Christmas**
    ### Dates: December 25

Christmas in Japan is not a total waste of time for someone used to Christmas in the West. You'll find lots of colorful lights and beautiful store displays. It seems that many Japanese have a tradition of eating Christmas cake. And of course, children look forward to receiving presents from Santa Claus.

- **New Year's holiday**
    ### Dates: January 1

New Year's is considered the biggest holiday in Japan, but since it's mainly a family holiday, it's not that exciting for visitors. The typical thing for a Japanese person to do is to line up in front of a shrine, sometimes for hours, to spend a few seconds praying the first prayer of the year. The roads and trains are crowded with people going back home. If you're not lucky enough to find someone to welcome you into their home, I'm sorry to say that New Year's in Japan can be a disappointment.

• Coming of Age Day ceremonies
Dates: the 2nd Sunday of January

Coming of Age Day ceremonies are held at civic centers and other halls on the second Monday of January. There, you'll see crowds of 20-year old men and women dressed in their finest kimono. It's a day to celebrate their advancement into adulthood. Usually, people born and raised in a given area participate in the ceremony. There you can see many happy classmates and teachers who helped students along the way reunite with each other. In Japan, the legal age to smoke and drink alcohol is 20, as is the voting age.

• Eat *nabe*

One of the most popular winter foods in Japan is *nabe*, which is basically a hot pot that that is placed in the center of the table that a group of people eats from together. Everyone picks out their own portion from the soup. It is cooked with ingredients like vegetables, fish and seafood in various kinds of soup stocks like soy sauce, *miso* or curry. It can really warm you up during the cold winter.

• Go skiing

There are some great ski resorts within a few hours from Tokyo. Rather than trying to arrange the trip yourself, it's probably best to talk to your hotel and ask them to make reservations on a tour bus that will take you to the resort in the morning and bring you back at night. The cost of these tours can be less than if you planned the trip yourself. Some popular ski spots near Tokyo include Echigo Yuzawa and Karuizawa.

• Go to an *onsen* (hot springs)

The idea of climbing naked into a bath with strangers might be a turn off, but you're missing something if you don't try it at least once. The most accessible one in central Tokyo is Spa LaQua at Tokyo Dome in Suidobashi. It's not really very traditional, but it's certainly enjoyable.

An *onsen* with a more traditional feel is Oedo-Onsen Monogatari in the Odaiba area. It may not be an *onsen* that's been around since ancient times, but it's modelled after those of the days when Tokyo was known as Edo, more than 200 years ago. Going there may make you feel like you've travelled back in time. On the Yurikamome Line, get off at the Telecom Center Station, and walk three minutes.

• See the Christmas lights

Tokyo has some really fantastic free "illuminations" (the Japanese word for Christmas lights). As a country, Japan doesn't celebrate Christmas as a religious holiday, but there are plenty of decorations. Great places for this include Shiodome, Shinjuku, Ginza, Roppongi Hills, Tokyo Midtown, Odaiba, Tokyo Dome City, Marunouchi, Omotesando, Akasaka Sacas and Yebisu Garden Place.

Christmas lights at Roppoingi Hills.

Here's how I would spend a nice winter day

Unless you're into self-torture, you'll want to take things slowly on a cold winter day. One area with a lot of indoor activities is Korakuen, located north of Suidobashi Station. I would get to Suidobashi Station at around 9:30 and go to Koishikawa Korakuen Garden. You'll need at least an hour to enjoy this beautiful garden. From there, you could take a short walk to the Tokyo Dome area.

Once you're there, you could go to an information window and ask about events. You're not guaranteed a ticket at the door, but events such as concerts at Tokyo Dome and professional wrestling and boxing at the

There's lots to see and do in the Tokyo Dome area.
663highland

Korakuen Hall are frequent. If you're interested, visit the space museum called TENQ where you can learn about space and even experience it.

If you'd like to get your thrills, try one of the amusement park rides. And then when you're ready for a rest, head to the Spa LaQua. It's more like a huge modern spa than a traditional Japanese hot springs you might have heard about, but it is relaxing. In the evening, you can stroll around the shopping mall there and choose from various kinds of cuisine to fit your mood.

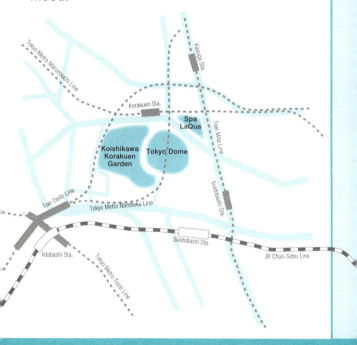

Spring and rainy season

Spring is the season Japanese look forward to because of, of course, cherry blossoms! The end of March and first two weeks of April is the season when the cherry blossoms usually come into bloom. In many parts of the world, April is considered the rainy season, but in Tokyo, April will bring some rain, but the real rainy season comes much later, around the middle of June.

The rainy season is unpredictable, and you'll probably want to take an umbrella with you no matter where you go. But there are actually some nice days, and some years are nicer than usual. And since a lot of visitors avoid the rainy season, if you're lucky, it can be a great time to visit.

- ## Kurayami Festival
  ### Dates: early May

This "Darkness Festival" at Okuni-Tama Jinja Shrine in Fuchu City is held around the beginning of May, and is one of the more bizarre festivals you'll find. The parade was originally held after dark, but it now starts at 6:00 p.m., finishing in time for you to catch a train back in central Tokyo.

• Sanja Festival
Dates: mid-May

Asakusa used to be a major center of Tokyo, but when it was not included on the Yamanote loop line, it risked becoming irrelevant. Fortunately, with the historical Senso-ji Temple—and the many annual events, Asakusa remains a worthwhile destination in Tokyo. If you can make it to the Sanja Festival in mid-May, you'll be seeing one of the three great festivals of Tokyo. The crowds are incredible, but that's part of the excitement!

• See cherry blossoms

When the cherry trees are blooming, Japanese go the parks to sit on the ground on tarps and hang out. It's the only time of the year you'll see anything like this, so it's a good time to people watch, while also enjoying the beautiful blossoms. You can see the blossoms almost anywhere you go in Tokyo, but there are a few places that deserve special mention.

One is Ueno Park near Ueno Station and the other is the river bank area. It's probably best to get off the train at Ichigaya Station and follow the crowds. The third—and probably the most famous—is Chidorigafuchi Koen near

Hanzomon Station and Kudanshita Station. Just get out of the station and follow the crowds to the moat around the Imperial Palace. Other hot spots include Inokashira Park near Kichijoji Station and Yoyogi Park near Harajuku Station.

• **Climb Mount Takao**

When you think about Tokyo, you think about tall buildings and large numbers of people, but you can escape all of that without actually leaving Tokyo if you go to Mount Takao, located about an hour from Shinjuku in the far west side of Tokyo. It's a great place to go hiking because of its easy access from the city, its natural beauty, and its cultural importance.

You can get half way up the mountain by taking a cable car to the 400-meter point, or by climbing. I recommend using the cable car and then hiking from there.

You can get to Takao-san-guchi Station in 45 minutes by using the Keio line Limited Express train from Shinjuku Station. From the station, there are plenty of signs written in English, or you can just follow the other hikers.

• **Go to a flea market**

In Japan, places where flea markets can be held regularly are limited. There are held frequently in Yoyogi park on weekends, but be sure to make sure when before you go. Since Japanese tend to take pretty good care of their clothes and other possessions, you can find a lot of great stuff at great prices. However, even if you don't buy anything, you may just want to enjoy the atmosphere. If you're like me, you love the idea of visiting a family's home to see how they live, but if that's not possible on your trip, a flea market is almost as good.

There will always be some professional flea market vendors, but most of the "shops" are set up by individuals trying to have a good time making a little cash. This is one of the few places in Tokyo where price haggling is expected. The site tokyocheapo.com has dates and related information.

• See outdoor performances

There aren't many outdoor venues in Tokyo, but some of the more notable ones are in Hibiya Park, Ueno Park and Yoyogi Park. You can see a wide range of performances including classical, jazz, world, Japanese traditional and popular music performances, along with dance, magic and much more. Most of the performances will be free and you can generally come and go freely.

Here's how I would spend a nice spring day

I would get up early and go to Hanzomon Station, and then walk around the moat. Near the Indian Embassy, there's a little boat rental business. If you wait for about an hour, you can take a little boat ride. If you're lucky, you'll get there at just the right time to enjoy floating in a carpet of blossoms on the water as you look up and watch pink snowflakes fall down on you.

From there, you might want to walk to the East Garden of the Imperial Palace, which is open to the public. It's a wonderful place to lie down on the grass and take a nap.

From there, I'd walk over to Yasukuni Shrine, dedicated to Japan's war dead. The shrine and the museum may put you in a somber mood, but it will certainly make you think. The cherry blossoms in the shrine are also beautiful, of course.

It's probably getting late by now, so you might want to walk to Tokyo Station. The tall buildings in front of the station have scores of restaurants, so it can be an especially nice place to have dinner before heading back to your hotel.

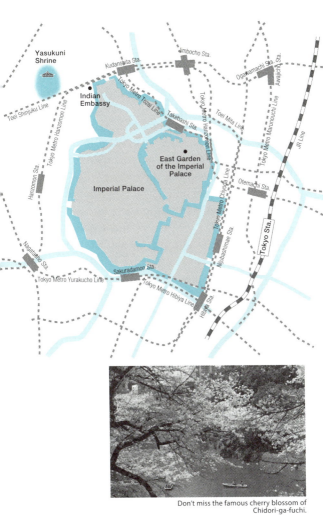

Don't miss the famous cherry blossom of Chidori-ga-fuchi.

Spring and rainy season 59

Summer

Two words will describe summers in Tokyo: hot and humid. While the daytime temperatures may hover around 35 degrees Celsius, you can expect humidity of up to 80 percent at times. In other words, you're going to sweat! Regardless, trains, restaurants and shops will sometimes overcompensate for the heat and keep the air-conditioning very low, so be prepared to sweat one minute and freeze the next! June is known as the rainy season, called *tsuyu* in Japanese, and that may extend into late July. In August you will see less rain, but much higher temperatures, sometimes reaching 40 degrees Celsius.

Summertime is the festival season in Tokyo, and there is some sort of festival going on almost every weekend. On any given day, you might find an art festival, film festival, beer festival or food festival, but you won't want to miss the more traditional festivals, either. Each part of Tokyo has its own way of celebrating the summer, but here are some of the more famous summer festivals.

• Asakusa Samba Carnival

Dates: the last Saturday of August

This isn't really a "festival," but became one of the more popular summer events since it was started in 1981. It may not compare to other carnivals around the world, but it is becoming more and more popular each year.

• Shinjuku Eisa Festival

Dates: the last Saturday of July

For some traditional Japanese dancing, check out the Eisa Festival. The crowds are smaller, and the event is more organized than other festivals or big events. Eisa is the name of a dance from Okinawa, the southern islands. It's an opportunity to listen to and experience the music and food of this unique region in Japan.

• Ueno Summer Festival

Dates: From mid-July to mid-August

During this period, you'll find events going on throughout the enormous Ueno Park. Highlights include the opening parade on the 17th and floating paper lanterns on the pond at 7:00 p.m. on July 17th. Along with performances at the stage near Shinobazunoike pond, you'll probably be able to catch a few street performances.

• *Tanabata* Festival (Star Festival)
Dates: the closest weekend to July

The closest weekend to July 7 is the time of the romantic *Tanabata* Festival—one of the most beautiful festivals in Japan. Many of the shopping districts will be decorated with colorful ornaments and wishes written on slips of paper tied to bamboo branches on display in front of many stores.

The Star Festival in Asagaya, a suburb of Tokyo.

• Sumida River Fireworks Festival
Dates: the last weekend of July

With roots dating back to 1733, the festival has become a must-see for summer visitors to Tokyo. In the evening, just walk towards Asakusa and you'll soon see where the crowds are gathering. The fireworks can also be seen from the higher floors of hotels and other buildings in the area.

• Go to beer gardens

A lot of people in Japan spend hot summer evenings cooling down with some beer. Throughout the city, on the rooftops of hotels and department stores, you'll find summer-only beer gardens that have cold beer and wonderful food. Many have an all-you-can-drink package, so this can be a special treat for big beer drinkers.

• Go to Comiket

If you're an anime or cosplay fan, then you probably already know about this "comic market" held in August and December at the Tokyo Big Sight convention center near the Kokusaitenjijo-seimon Station and Kokusaitenjijo Station. Even if you're not a big fan, it can still be a great place to explore Japanese subculture and see some top-class art in the form of comics and costumes.

Fireworks over Sumida river.

Here's how I would spend a nice summer day

For a great summer day in Tokyo, I'd go to Ueno Park and take in a couple museums. There are in fact five museums in the park that cover many areas from traditional art, modern art, and even a huge science museum, so there's lots of places to get out of the heat.

Then, I'd have a pizza at the little shop near the main entrance of the zoo. After that, I'd head to the Shitamachi Museum, located in the southwest side of Ueno Park. This often overlooked museum takes you back about 100 years. About 30 minutes is enough time to see everything, or you can spend longer playing old-fashioned games.

The Shitamachi Museum is dedicated to the traditional culture of Tokyo.

From there, I recommend going to the old-fashioned Ameyoko shopping street located in a southeasterly direction from the park. You'll find plenty of places to choose for dinner before heading back to your hotel.

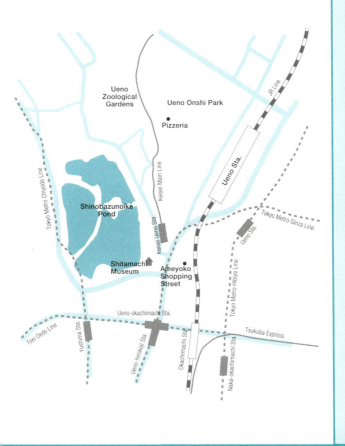

Autumn

Just like spring, autumn is a wonderful season to visit Tokyo, especially mid-October to mid-November, when it's cool and not too cold. Nights can be a little chilly, but a jacket is usually enough. From late November, you might need a coat and gloves, but it's not likely at all to snow.

- ### Harajuku-Omotesando Hello Halloween Pumpkin Parade

  Dates: the last Sunday of October

In Japan, it's said that summer is the season for listening to ghost stories and when the spirits of one's ancestors return to visit their homes, but Halloween in autumn has now come to be completely accepted. One Japanese interpretation of Halloween is the big Halloween Parade, usually on the last Sunday of October. As you can imagine, Japanese with years of experience doing cosplay can do Halloween better than anyone else.

- ### Saury Festival in Meguro

  Dates: the first Sunday of September

Saury, a seasonal fish of autumn, is very

popular in Japan. Saury is generally lightly salted, grilled then eaten with *sudachi* or grated *daikon* radish. At this event, festival-goers are treated to free charcoal grilled saury. You'll have to wait in line, but eating fresh saury under the autumn sky is more than worth it.

• Pick up some nuts that smell like...

When going for a walk in Tokyo, you might get hit by a smell that will remind you of...um... an open sewer, to put it nicely. But you might also see people gathered around picking up "droppings" from the ground—but they're not what you think. They're picking up seeds from the gingko trees that have a terrible smell. If you wanted to harvest them yourself, you'd have to take them back to your hotel and wash off the stinky pulp in your room, and then you'd probably get kicked out for stinking up the place. But you might see them on the menu during this season—they're delicious.

• Visit one of the many public gardens

During feudal times, powerful warlords used to have enormous estates in Tokyo, but during modernization, the estates became the property of the government, and the result is some beautiful park-like gardens—beautiful in all seasons, but perhaps especially so in the autumn. Here are some of the more impressive ones:

○ Shinjuku Gyoen

Includes a French-style garden and Japanese landscaped garden with lots of grass and beautiful ponds.

○ Rikugien

Arguably the most beautiful classical Japanese garden in Tokyo. Scenes are reproduced from famous poems in the design of the garden.

○ Hama Rikyu Garden

A beautiful and historic Japanese garden alongside Tokyo Bay near Hamamatsucho Station (Yamanote Line). Famous for its ancient trees.

○ Kyu Shiba Rikyu Garden

Surrounded by skyscrapers, this spacious garden is known for its man-made hills.

○ Inokashira Park

Located near Kichijoji Station on the Chuo

Line, this expansive park is a wonderful way to spend a pleasant afternoon, and you might also check out the fashionable shops on the other side of the station.

○ **Yoyogi Park** (Refer to page 98)

○ **Koishikawa Korakuen** (Refer to page 52)

• **Visit a museum**

One place to go that has many museums in one place is Ueno Park. There you'll find museums of modern art, traditional Japan, world-class traveling exhibitions and even science.

Located in Minami Aoyama, Minato-ku, is the Taro Okamoto Memorial Museum, where you can view the work of Taro Okamoto, an artist often regarded as Japan's Picasso. The building was the artist's personal studio and dwelling until he passed away in 1996 at the age of 84. There is also a cafe called *a Piece of Cake* located in the building, where a garden displays his work, and you can appreciate the work while enjoying coffee or cake.

Here's how I would spend a nice autumn day

I would go to Asakusa in the morning and walk around Senso-ji Temple, and then walk across the river to Tokyo Skytree. As long as you walk towards the huge tower you won't get lost. After walking around the tower, if the sky is clear, you might want to go up to the top of the tower. Same-day tickets for the viewing deck at 350 meters high cost 2,060 yen for adults. If you choose to continue up to the viewing corridor at 450 meters high it will cost an extra 1,030 yen.

From the tower, cross the nearby river using the bridge that goes to Asakusa. You should be able to see the wharf where you can board a river ferry. You can use the ferry to go to a variety of places, or just take a round trip and return to Asakusa. I also recommend going to Hamarikyu Garden (open from 9:00 a.m. to 5:00 p.m.) and walking around the gardens that once surrounded the villa of the important Tokugawa family shogunate in the 17th century.

From there, you could walk 15 minutes to Hamamatsu Station on the Yamanote Line and call it a day, or you could get back on the ferry and go to a number of other places like the Tokyo Sea Life Park (Kasai Rinkai Park Wharf), which is especially fun for children, or the National Museum of Emerging Science and Innovation (Palette Town Wharf), perfect for curious types.

The river ferry is a great way to enjoy Tokyo Bay.

Senso-ji Temple
Sumida River
Tokyo Metro Ginza Line
Asakusa Sta.
Asakusa Sta.
Tobu Skytree Line
River ferry boarding point
Toei Asakusa Line
Tokyo Skytree Sta.
Honjo-azumabashi Sta.
Oshiage Sta. 'SKYTREE'
Tokyo Metro Hanzomon Line

To Tokyo/Ueno
Hamarikyu Garden
Hinode Pier
Toyosu
Tokyo Big Sight
Palette Town Wharf
Odaiba Seaside Park
Hamamatsucho Sta.

Autumn 71

The Places

- List of Railway Lines in Chapter 3 & 4

    - Y   Yamanote Line
    - S   Subway (Toei & Tokyo Metro)
    - T   Tobu Isesaki Line
    - Ke   Keisei Main Line
    - N   Nippori-Toneri Liner
    - Yu   Yurikamome Line
    - R   Rinkai Line
    - J   JR Line (except Yamanote Line)
    - K   Keio Line
    - E   Enoden Line
    - O   Odakyu Line
    - M   Tokyo Monorail

Asakusa Area

Senso-ji Temple, Kappabashi Dogu Street, Tokyo Skytree

Keywords:
- Older and more traditional area of Tokyo
- Temples and shrines
- Fine art museums

When visitors to Japan only have time to see one thing, this is often where they're told to go. It's a fun place to experience tradition, arts, shopping, people watching and delicious food all within a small area. This is the area generally called *shitamachi*. That's best translated as "traditional residential area." It also includes interesting architecture, shopping and museums.

When Tokyo was founded around 1600, this part of the city near waterways and the ocean was the center. Growth towards westward and reclamation of the Tokyo Bay area changed that, but this area with left with much of its old-Japan feel. If you're energetic and rent a bicycle, then it's possible to see this entire area in one day. But you might want to take one day each for the Asakusa area and the Ueno area.

• Senso-ji Temple
S Asakusa

Senso-ji Temple and the all of the many covered shopping streets surrounding it are well worth a visit. When visitors only have a few hours to spend in Tokyo, they usually go to Asakusa. The temple complex is one of the oldest in Tokyo, and it's a good place to see many different types of traditional architecture in one area.

Everyone has to visit Senso-ji, an ancient temple in Asakusa.

• Kappabashi Dogu Street
S Tawaramachi

This is where you can find every utensil and tool for the kitchen. There are dozens of stores there selling such utensils. Even if you don't buy anything, it's still fun to look around. The very edible-looking wax food models are especially popular. You can walk there in about 10 minutes from Senso-ji Temple.

Kappabashi-dori known for having every utensil and tool you need for the kitchen.

• Tokyo Skytree
T Tokyo Skytree; **S** Oshiage

This is one of the tallest structures in Asia at 634 meters tall. Those who enjoy walking can trek there from Senso-ji by taking the bridge over the Sumida River, otherwise you can take the Tobu Skytree Line and get off at Tokyo Skytree Station. You can go to the top of the tower for a great view of the city on clear days, or you can go to the shopping center at the base of the tower and spend some time seeing the trendy new stores there.

This tower in Sumida is now a popular destination for many tourists.

If I were you, I would...

Rent a bicycle. Just get off at the North Exit at JR Okachimachi Station, turn right and walk for 50 meters to the big intersection. There's a bicycle rental shop right under the intersection. The surrounding area is mostly flat, so it's easy to go almost anywhere on a bike. It's also much cheaper and quicker, and you can see more than if you just rode the train.

From here, by bicycle you can see a lot of interesting parts of Tokyo including Ueno

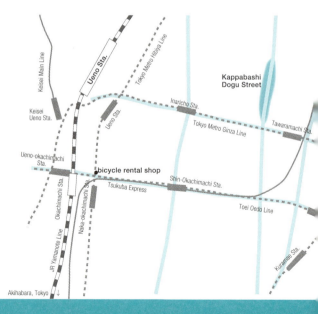

Park, Akihabara, Otemachi, Tokyo Station, the Imperial Palace, Ginza and Tsukiji—just ask for an English map when you rent the bicycle.

But today, let's head towards Asakusa, stopping first at Kappabashi Street to check out the kitchen supplies. From there, you're only about 10 minutes away from Senso-ji Temple. You'll need to get off your bike and walk around to really enjoy the sites.

After you've had your fill of Asakusa, you can either check out the huge Tokyo Skytree on the other side of the river, or just ride along the bank of the Sumida River, exploring the area as you go.

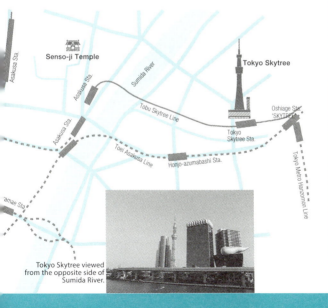

Tokyo Skytree viewed from the opposite side of Sumida River.

Asakusa Area 79

Ueno Area

Yanesen, Ueno Onshi Park, Ameyoko, Akihabara Electronics City

Keywords:
- Traditional residential area
- Huge park and zoo
- Akihabara Electric Town and subculture

Ueno Park and the surrounding area is a part of Tokyo that has managed to maintain many of the old structures and the atmosphere of days past. The park itself shows the remnants of the aristocratic and scholarly classes in the form of old temples and shrines, while the area around the park retains the feel of the commoner classes with shops bunched together and maze-like streets and walkways.

• Yanesen

Y **Ke** **N** Nippori; **S** Sendagi; **S** Nezu

Yanesen is the nickname for an area that includes YAnaka, NEzu and SENdagi. Tokyo is becoming more and more of a cement jungle with each year, but this area lags a little behind the rest of the city in terms of urban development. It contains an old residential area of Tokyo, making it a favorite destination with visitors to Japan.

Many guidebooks will tell you about the picturesque Yanaka Ginza shopping street and the serene Nezu Shrine, but the best thing there are the many narrow alleys that lead off of the main roads. You could easily spend a full day wandering around getting lost—which is the best way to see Yanesen!

Yanaka, a part of Tokyo where the old residential atomosphere survives.

I recommend getting off at Nippori Station and heading west. That will get you to the Yanaka Ginza shopping street. At the bottom of the street, turn left and then just explore. You'll eventually want to head to Nezu Shrine. From there, you can keep going southward and you'll eventually get to Ueno Zoo and Ueno Park. It's probably possible to visit Yanesen, Ueno Zoo, Ueno Park and maybe even Akihabara in a day—but this is also a great place to spend one of your easygoing days.

- **Ueno Onshi Park**

Y S Ueno

This is where you can find some of the best museums in Japan, an enormous zoo, and a great science museum. This is a great place to go with a family or group because there's something for everyone there. You can also walk around and see some temples and shrines and some really amazing street performers.

A spacious public park and center of culture in Tokyo.

- **Ameyoko**

Y S Ueno; Y Okachimachi

This enormous, crowded shopping area is sometimes called Tokyo's kitchen because of all the shops selling cooking ingredients. You can buy almost anything imaginable here.

- **Akihabara Electronics City**

Y S Akihabara

In addition to offering computers, cameras and almost every other gadget you can imagine, it has also become one of the main centers of Japanese pop culture. Most of the electronics streets are to the left of the main Chuo Street, but there are shops almost everywhere you go. Visit a "maid cafe" to be served by young women who will make you feel special with sweet smiles and sweet talk. Just talk to one of the many "maids" along the street looking for clients and she'll show you where to go. You can get to Akihabara by walking from Ueno Park or taking a three-minute train ride on the JR Yamanote Line. I recommend walking.

Ameyoko, between Ueno and Okachimachi stations is filled with tiny shops echoing the blackmarket days after WWII.

If I were you, I would...

Get off at Ueno Station and go to the Tokyo Metropolitan Art Museum, where you can see both traditional Japanese and Western works of art. If the weather is good, it might even be nice to head to Ueno Zoo and see the famous pandas. After that, I'd walk southwest to the lower level of the park and head to the *Shitamachi* Museum.

After that, walk east to the Ameyoko area on either side of the JR line's raised tracks. If you walk straight along these tracks past Okachimachi Station, it'll lead you right to Akihabara Station. If I were you, I'd walk on the left side of the line. Under the train line, you'll find a lot of interesting shops, but don't miss the art galleries and shops in the 2k540 AKI-OKA ARTISAN area.

From there, try to follow the tracks until you come across an interesting grocery store that sells local food from all over Japan and

The Akihabara electronic district is the center of *otaku* and *anime* culture.

offers a lot of free samples. Then go a few more steps towards Akihabara Station and you'll find some exciting themed cafes with loud music and, most likely, lines of people waiting to get in. Then, set out to explore Akihabara Electric Town.

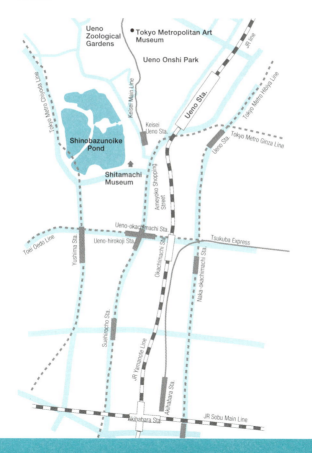

Tokyo Station Area

Tokyo Station Building, Otemachi, The Imperial Palace, Ginza, The Kabuki-za Theater, Nihonbashi, Tsukiji Fish Market

Keywords:
- History and tradition
- Beautiful architecture
- The center of Tokyo

It has been hundreds of years since the Emperor of Japan has had true political power. When he was moved from Kyoto to Tokyo about 400 years ago, a palace was built not far from the shores of Tokyo Bay.

Over the years, the distance between the palace and the bay has grown as the bay has been filled in to create more space for building. So this is the area to discover the historical roots of Japanese government and business.

• Tokyo Station Building
Y S Tokyo; **Y S** Otemachi

Much of the enormous red-brick station was destroyed in during WWII. While most station buildings you'll see are recent structures built mostly for convenience, Tokyo Station, finished after the war in 1945, has retained (or recovered) it's original grandeur.

Post-war repairs focused on making it reusable, but a remodeling project completed in 2013 has made the building more impressive than ever. As you pass through it, make sure you take the time to look up and around at this example of early Western architecture in Japan.

Tokyo Station, near the Imperial Palace, is one of the busiest and most beautiful stations in Japan.

The newly renovated Tokyo Station building.

• Otemachi
Y S Otemachi

This is the area between Tokyo Station and the Imperial Palace. The walk from the station to the palace takes about 10 minutes, but you should walk around and see the impressive office buildings and shops in the area. While Otemachi used to be only a business district, it has transformed in recent years into a popular place for tourists and shoppers.

• The Imperial Palace
Y S Tokyo; Y S Otemachi

The Palace is both impressive and simplistic. It covers a huge area right in the middle of Tokyo, but casual visitors can only enter certain parts of it. Runners love to run the five-kilometer road around the palace, but I suggest going to Higashi Gyoen (East Garden).

The East Garden is now mostly void of structures and you can see a beautiful Japanese garden there, but it used to be covered in buildings related to the Shogun government and Imperial family, and as of this writing, there is talk about reconstructing some of these old buildings in time for the 2020 Olympics—so maybe there will be a lot more to see and do here in the future. For now, it's a great place to enjoy a beautiful Japanese garden and also to take a nap on the well-kept lawn.

The main bridge to the Imperial Palace is nicknamed Nijubashi.

The old stone walls are still very impressive. If you go there expecting a Buckingham Palace experience, you may find things a little more toned down than European-style palaces. You may even think that the really beautiful areas are hidden from the public eye, but I have been inside, and while it's very beautiful, I assure you it's not as beautiful as the parts visible to the public. If, however, you go to the Imperial Palace hoping to see a wonderful example of Japan's sense of simple beauty, you won't be disappointed.

The historic Sakuradamon Gate.

• Ginza
Y S Ginza; Y S Tokyo; Y S Yurakucho

Ginza is located on the eastern side of Tokyo Station, while the Imperial Palace is on the western side. You can walk there from the station, or take a short taxi ride. Ginza is the premier shopping area of Tokyo with brand-name shops from around the world.

But even if you're not a big-time shopper, you can still enjoy window-shopping. It's also a great place to splurge at one of the many stylish Japanese or Western confectionery

Ginza 4-chome intersection in the heart of Ginza.

shops. If you go there on Sunday, the main street is closed to cars so pedestrians can enjoy a leisurely stroll.

• **The Kabuki-za Theater**
S Higashi-ginza

This theater is located on the eastern side of Ginza near the Higashi-Ginza subway station. If you're in the area around noon, you can drop in and see a matinee performance. It's something you won't see anywhere else and one of the premier places for kabuki performances in all of Japan.

There are two different daily productions: the matinee (11:00 to 3:45) and the evening performance (4:30 to 9:00). You can make reservations several days ahead by calling the phone number 0570-000-489 (English available) to reserve your tickets.

However, if you don't know whether kabuki is your thing or not, get the cheapest tickets so you can watch a single act from the 4th floor gallery. These tickets go on sale on the day of the performance, but try to get there early as they often sell out fast.

Rebuilt in 2013, Ginza's Kabuki Theater is the center of this traditional performance art.

• Nihonbashi
S Nihombashi

Nihonbashi doesn't get the attention that Ginza gets, but there was a day when it was the center of Tokyo and Japan. In fact, when the Nihonbashi Bridge was built in 1603, it was the starting point for five major highways. The bridge itself is now located under an overbearing expressway, but it stills retains the grandeur of the 1911 version.

Nihonbashi, literally meaning Japan Bridge, was the center of business in the Edo Period.

There are a lot of great sites here that you won't want to miss in this area. One of my favorites is the Bridgestone Museum of Art. If you like waiting in lines, there are plenty of other places to choose from, but this often forgotten museum includes works by artists as well-known as Rembrandt, Picasso and Warhol without the usual crowds.

Nowadays, Nihonbashi is famous among Japanese mostly for shopping, especially the Mitsukoshi Department Store. The current building, with its ornate architecture, was constructed in 1935, but the business itself dates back to 1673.

This is another great place to go for a walk and get lost. It won't be hard at all to find traditional Japanese-style shops, old forgotten buildings and other remnants of days bygone.

• Tsukiji Fish Market
🆂 Tsukiji

The largest fish market in the world is just to the south of the kabuki theater, so you can get there on foot in about 10 minutes. If you go there in the afternoon, it'll seem almost abandoned, so you'll want to go to Tsukiji in the morning—the earlier the better. It's the biggest fish market in Japan, and one of the largest in the world. You can walk around the many little shops to find fresh fish and much more—almost any ingredient or item related to Japanese cuisine.

Get there early in the morning, around 5:00 a.m. if possible, and you can even see the famous tuna auction. Only 120 visitors are allowed into the tuna auction. You'll need to apply at the *Osakana Fukyu* Center (Fish Information Center) at the Kachidoki Gate, starting from 5:00 a.m. The first group of 60 visitors is admitted from 5:25, and a second group is admitted at around 5:50. This place is like a busy factory, so be very careful where you walk, and try not to get in the way of workers.

Tsukiji is one of the largest wholesale fish, furit and vegetable markets in the world.

If I were you, I would...

Try to get to the Tsukiji Fish Market a little before 5:00 a.m., and make reservations for the Tuna auction at the Kachidoki Gate. After a couple of hours or so of wandering around, I'd have sushi for breakfast, and then I'd walk to the Hongan-ji Temple. This is a rather unusual temple made of cement, but inside you'll find chairs and a quiet atmosphere to rest and calm your mind.

From there, I would walk to Higashi-Ginza (10 minutes) and enjoy one act of the kabuki matinee performance. After the kabuki performance, walk a little further west to reach Ginza's main street, where you can shop and have lunch.

Next, head to the East Garden of the Imperial Palace (30 minutes by foot or 15 by taxi). After you've enjoyed walking around there, head back to Tokyo Station, but don't forget check out the huge office buildings of Otemachi. The buildings closest to the station are filled with restaurants and other shops, so you'll have hundreds of places to choose from for dinner. If you go higher up in the buildings, you can enjoy a great view of the city.

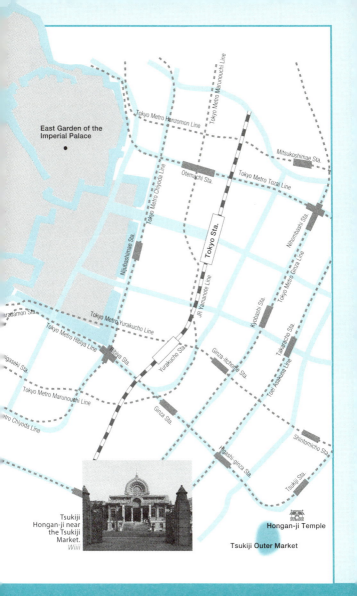

Shibuya Area

Shibuya Station and surrounding areas, SHIBUYA 109, Shibuya Scramble Crossing, Yoyogi Park, Meiji Shrine, Harajuku Station and surrounding area

Keywords:
- Youth culture
- Nightlife
- Entertainment

In the formative years of the city of Tokyo, which was originally called Edo, the areas near the bay became populated first. People moved into the surrounding areas much later. After the Yamanote loop train line was completed in 1925, the western side of Tokyo started to grow, and now Shibuya and Shinjuku are perhaps the two busiest parts of Tokyo. Shibuya is especially popular with the younger generations.

You can get to Shibuya on the Yamanote Line, but there are also many other lines, including subway lines, that will get you there as well. To get from Shibuya to Shinjuku, take the Yamanote Line, as for Harajuku, you can easily get there on foot from Shibuya.

Visitors to Japan love to take pictures at Shibuya's hectic scramble intersection.

- **Shibuya Station and surrounding areas**
Y S Shibuya

The area around Shibuya Station has become famous for being a place to shop and party. Instead of going to a particular point in Shibuya, it's probably better to start on one side of the station, and just walk around and explore.

- **SHIBUYA109**
Y S Shibuya

The most famous of the many shopping centers is probably SHIBUYA109 with its under-30 fashion. Trendy is the only type of fashion you'll find here—which can be said about most of Shibuya. The pedestrian street on the side of SHIBUYA109 is called Center Gai (Center Street). As the name indicates, it's the center of everything that makes Shibuya Shibuya.

- **Shibuya Scramble Crossing**
Y S Shibuya

This crossing, located outside the eastern exists of the station—near the Hachiko Exit—has become famous for being completely chaotic. When the lights for pedestrians turn green, people from the four corners all rush across the street, somehow avoiding running into each other. This is one of the most photographed spots in Tokyo.

• Yoyogi Park
Y Harajuku; **S** Yoyogi-koen;
S Meiji-jingumae 'Harajuku'

If you walk North from the Shibuya shopping streets, you'll get to Yoyogi Park. On weekends, there will probably be a flea market or festival of some sort going on in the part of the park closest to Shibuya, but after you cross the busy streets, you'll go into the heart of Yoyogi Park and find yourself in a more quiet and relaxing part of Tokyo.

Although there are lots of grass and trees, the most interesting thing is the creative young people that gather there. You can probably find an impromptu performance by a musician or street performer. It's one of the few places in Tokyo where you can play Frisbee or just lie down on the grass and take a nap. The northern side of the park has more nature while the area near Harajuku Station is more lively and entertaining. On weekends, you'll probably see a 1950s American rock-and-roll dance group that draws huge crowds with their fancy moves and greased hair—lots of fun!

- **Meiji Shrine**

Y Harajuku; **S** Meiji-jingumae 'Harajuku'

The shrine itself is not extremely fancy, but combined with the surrounding park grounds of Meiji Shrine, it's worth the visit. The park is 700,000 square-meters, but most of it is forest, with 170,000 trees of a few hundred different species. Keep walking and you'll eventually get to a huge grassy area where you can lie down under a tree, so bring something to lay on. The contrast of the lush greens with the high-rise buildings in the background is amazing.

- **Harajuku Station and surrounding area**

Y Harajuku; **S** Meiji-jingumae 'Harajuku'

Harajuku Station has two exits: the Takeshita Exit takes you directly to a narrow shopping street for pedestrians only, and if you turn right out of the Omotesando Exit, the road will take you to Yoyogi Park and Meiji Shrine. If you turn left, it will take you to Omotesando.

Takeshita Street is known for being a fashion hub for younger generations. It's where the young and fashionably eccentric gather.

Omotesando serves a slightly older crowd with famous designer boutiques. Harajuku is a fun place to shop, but it's also a great place to go people watching.

If I were you, I would...

Go to the Omotesando exit of Harajuku Station in the morning and walk a minute or two across the bridge over the tracks to the entrance of Meiji Shrine. I'd spend an hour or two walking through the park. You might even be able to catch a wedding or some other traditional ceremony.

Then, I'd head back to the station and go to the entrance of Yoyogi Park, without going back over the bridge. There are a lot of interesting people and culture to be seen near the entrance.

From there, I'd head back to Harajuku Station, and find the small Takeshita-dori street that starts from the North (Takeshita) Exit. There should be lots to see on this street—a major pop culture spot.

When you get to the main road called Meiji-dori, you could turn left and in about a minute walk to the entrance of Togo Shrine. It's much, much smaller than Meiji Shrine, but it's packed with beauty.

If you turn right onto Meiji-dori and walk for about one minute, and you'll reach a large intersection. This is where Meiji-dori and Omotesando meet. The streets nearby make up one of the largest fashion areas in Tokyo. If you're into fashion, turn left and go towards the Omotesando Hills fashion center.

Or you can skip that and go right back toward Harajuku Station. Go across the bridge and keep going until you see a park area to your left. Cross the street and go through the park, moving south toward Shibuya Station. In a few minutes, you'll be in busy Shibuya. You won't have any trouble finding interesting and fun places to eat and shop till you drop!

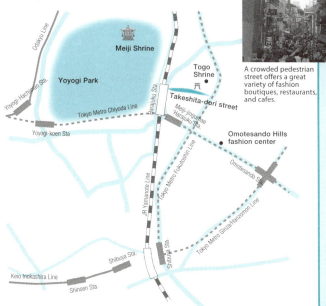

A crowded pedestrian street offers a great variety of fashion boutiques, restaurants, and cafes.

Shinjuku Area

Western Shinjuku, Eastern Shinjuku, Kabukicho, 2-chome gay district, Shinjuku Gyoen National Garden, Southern Shinjuku, Shin-Okubo

Keywords:
- Young culture
- Skyscrapers
- Nightlife
- Entertainment

In many ways, Shinjuku is the heart of Tokyo. It is the busiest station in Tokyo by far; the JR Line alone is used by more than 700,000 passengers a day. Trying to get through the station can be a hassle, but it's also the main transfer point to many other train lines.

• Western Shinjuku

Y S Shinjuku; **S** Shinjuku-nishiguchi

The western side has sky-high office buildings, so if you're interested in architecture, it's a fun place to wander around. But right in between all of these modern buildings is Omoide-yokocho—more commonly called Shomben-yokocho, or Piss Alley. This little bar area is located on the western side of the station to the north. Although you hopefully won't see anyone actually urinating, you will be able to enjoy exploring narrow paths with all sorts of little bars and delicious morsels of *yakitori* and other treats.

The Tokyo Metropolitan Government Building in Shinjuku with a free observaion deck.

• Eastern Shinjuku
Y S Shinjuku; S Higashi-shinjuku

The eastern side is a little wilder. It has several famous bar areas, tons of places for shopping and everything you'd expect to find in Tokyo.

• Kabukicho
Y S Shinjuku; S Higashi-shinjuku

Kabukicho is the most famous and notorious bar area of Tokyo. I wouldn't recommend going there alone. This area has all the shadier sites of a major city, and while you're probably safe walking around there even at night, you never know what might happen at the local bars and pubs.

Kabukicho features countless restaurants, bars nightclubs.

Shinjuku Area

Golden Gai, between Kabukicho and Hanazono Shrine, is the older bar area. It has six small paths lined with almost 200 tiny bars big enough for six or seven people at a time.

• 2-chome gay district
Y S Shinjuku; **S** Higashi-shinjuku

If you walk almost directly East of Shinjuku Station, you'll get to Shinjuku 2-chome. This area is famous for its gay bars and shops. People of various sexual orientations might enjoy exploring the area.

• Shinjuku Gyoen National Garden
Y S Shinjuku; **S** Shinjuku-gyoemmae;
S Shinjuku-sanchome

Not far from 2-chome is a huge park that's a great place to escape the crazy atmosphere of Shinjuku. You can easily spend an hour enjoying the beautiful gardens, or much longer taking a nap on the grass or viewing the cherry blossom trees if they're in bloom. It's a short walk from Shinjuku Station, but you can also catch the Marunouchi Line to Shinjuku-gyoemmae Station. Park hours are 9:30 to 16:00, and admission is 200 yen for adults and 50 yen for children.

• Southern Shinjuku
Y S Shinjuku; **S** Shinjuku-sanchome

On the southern side of Shinjuku Station is a modern shopping mall called Takashimaya Times Square, which has a huge department store and book store. It also carries a wide range of both Japanese and international clothing brands and has three floors of great restaurants. It's a fun place to spend a few hours, especially if the weather is bad.

• Shin-Okubo
Y Shin-Okubo; **Y S** Shinjuku

If you don't have time to go to Korea on this trip, then you can just go to Shin-Okubo. This area has evolved into a Little Korean town with everything Korean you can imagine. You'll probably be able to pick up an English map near the station that shows many of the Korean shops, but it might be easier to just follow the crowds. You'll find grocery stores and restaurants, but there are also more than a few Korean-style cafes that have a different feel than Japanese cafes. There are so many Korean shops and Korean speakers you'll forget you're in Japan!

If I were you, I would...

Get up early and go to Shinjuku Gyoen. After enjoying an hour or so in the park, head back to the station. The area between the park and the station has hundreds of shops to explore. With hundreds of restaurants to choose from everywhere you go in Shinjuku, it's a great place to have lunch. Once you're done eating, walk north towards Shin-Okubo Station. You'll probably end up passing through the Kabukicho area. During the day, it's quite different from what it looks like at night, and it might be worth spending some time wandering around.

When you get to the Korean area, you'll know you're there because many of the signs will be in Korean. If you haven't eaten lunch or if you're still hungry, you can try some Korean food, or

Enjoy Korean food in the area near Shin-Okubo Station.

just relax at one of the Korean cafes. If you still have some energy and are feeling adventurous, head back to Kabukicho, if you have the money, you'll be able to find something to do until the next morning.

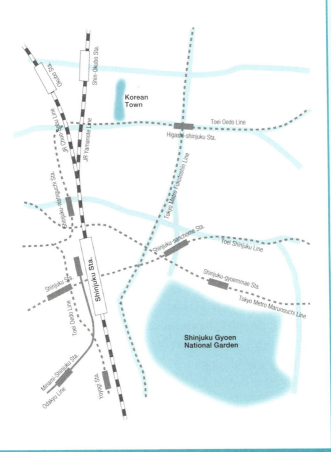

Akasaka / Roppongi / Azabu Area

Roppongi Hills, Tokyo Midtown, Nogi Shrine and General Nogi's Residence, The National Art Center, Akasaka Hikawa Shrine

Keywords:
- nightlife
- shopping
- art museums

After World War II, Roppongi became known as the location where the military forces and foreign bureaucrats lived because of its location near the Diet Building. It wasn't long before businesses catering to this community started to appear, and the area soon became the known as the best place to go to party. Over the years, huge shopping centers and office complexes have made it one of the best places to experience modern Japan.

• Roppongi Hills
S Roppongi; S Azabu-juban; S Nogizaka

This is an enormous complex where you could easily spend an entire day that might include a visit to the Mori Art Museum and the enormous Mori Arts Center Gallery on the 52nd floor, with outlets offering things ranging from fashion and cinema to modern and historical paintings. And while you're up on the 52nd floor, you'll want to spend time in the beautiful observation deck.

Back on the ground floor, the Roppongi Hills Arena is an open space where you can find live events and performances. It's a great place to chill before or after catching a movie at the TOHO Cinemas Roppongi Hills.

Roppongi Hills has everything: corporate offices, apartments, hotels, shops, restaurants, movie theaters, a museum and parks.

• **Tokyo Midtown**
S Roppongi; S Nogizaka

Built on a huge plot of land owned by the Defense Agency, this complex contains the tallest building in Tokyo, along with a park-like area that takes up about half of the grounds. The Midtown Tower is 248 meters tall, and the top floors are occupied by a 5-star Ritz Carlton Hotel. The lower floors are occupied by some of the top companies in Japan and the world. The shopping area on the lower floors has high-end clothing shops as well as classy cafes and restaurants.

Akasaka / Roppongi / Azabu Area

Two must-see spots here are the Suntory Museum of Art, with its stunning paintings, ceramics, lacquerware, glassware, dyeing and weaving, and the Fujifilm Square—exhibiting everything related to photography.

- **Nogi Shrine and General Nogi's Residence**

S Nogizaka

Less than 10 minutes by foot from Tokyo Midtown, this is a great place to take a break from the modern atmosphere. The shrine is serene, while the small house is interesting and full of history. Open to the public only on September 12 and 13, this is where the famous General Nogi and his wife killed themselves in a suicide ritual upon the death of the Emperor Meiji in 1912.

The quiet Nogi Shrine near Roppongi Hills. *Rs1421*

- **The National Art Center**

S Roppongi; S Nogizaka

Opened in 2007, this is the largest art museum in Tokyo and is widely known for its modern design with waves of glass. While there is no permanent art collection, the museum features the latest trends in art from around the world. You might also want to sit in on an art lecture, symposia, presentation or workshop, or just take it easy at one of the cafes.

The National Art Center in Roppongi.

• Akasaka Hikawa Shrine
S Roppongi; S Nogizaka

This is another great place to get away from the hustle and bustle. It's considered one of the 10 most important Shinto shrines in Tokyo, and also one of the most relaxing places in the city with beautiful trees and greenery. Those with an interest in architecture will want to take note of the unique traditional structures.

The quaint Akasaka Hikawa Shrine. *Chiether*

If I were you, I would...

Take the Chiyoda Line and get off at Nogizaka Station. From there, you can go directly to the National Art Center through a tunnel. You'll want to spend a couple of hours there before going for a walk around the Nogi Shrine and General Nogi's Residence. Maybe a little after the noon-time rush, arrive at Tokyo Midtown for a late lunch. After that, you can spend an hour or so wandering around the museums and the grounds. An hour or so before the sun

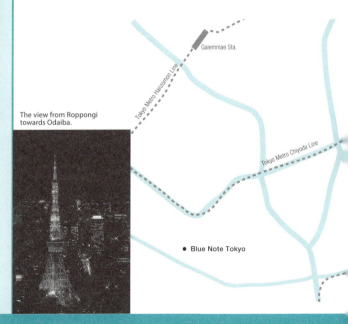

The view from Roppongi towards Odaiba.

starts to set, head toward Roppongi Hills and go to the 52nd-floor observation deck. If you time it right, and the weather cooperates, you'll see what might be one of the most beautiful sunsets of your life.

If you have the energy and the interest, you can walk around the backstreets near Roppongi Station. Wherever you go, people will try to pull you into their shop, but they can easily be ignored. If money's not an issue, I'd spend the final hours of the day at the famous Blue Note Tokyo jazz club.

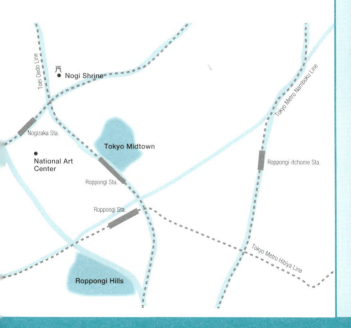

Akasaka / Roppongi / Azabu Area

Odaiba Area

Rainbow Bridge, Aqua City Odaiba, Panasonic Center, The National Museum of Emerging Science and Innovation Miraikan, Museum of Maritime Science, Odaiba Seaside Park, *Daikanransha* Ferris wheel, VenusFort, Fuji TV Station, Megaweb, Toyota City Showcase, Oedo-Onsen Monogatari

Keywords:
- Family friendly
- Science and technology
- Shopping
- Beach

From its earliest days, Tokyo has been expanding by filling in the bay to create more land. In fact, old maps of the city show the Imperial Palace just minutes away from the ocean, but now it's many times further away. An especially ambitious project is the Odaiba area in the Tokyo Bay.

To get there, get on the Yurikamome Line from the Shinbashi Yamanote station. One of the best parts of the trip is the short train ride across the bay on the Rainbow Bridge, so get your camera out.

The Rainbow Bridge crossing northern Tokyo Bay.

• Rainbow Bridge

Visible from almost anywhere in the bay area, this huge and beautiful suspension bridge was opened in 1993. It's especially impressive at night when it's lit up. It carries three transportation lines on two decks, including the Yurikamome Line.

• Aqua City Odaiba
Yu Daiba; **R** Tokyo Teleport

With over 50 unique restaurants with cuisine from around the world, Odaiba's Aqua City is perfect for people who like food. Don't miss the Ramen Kokugikan theme park. If you have time, you can even catch a movie at the Odaiba Cinema Mediage with 13 screens.

Find almost any kind of restaurant at Aqua City. *ITA-ATU*

• Panasonic Center
Yu Ariake; **R** Kokusai-tenjijo

The global electronics manufacturer showcases its vision of the future here, so it's fun to get a look at what the future home might look like.

It's something every technology geek will want to see.

• The National Museum of Emerging Science and Innovation (Miraikan)
Yu Telecom Center; **R** Tokyo Teleport

This is another place to go to get a glimpse at Japan's cutting-edge science and technology on five different floors of the museum. It's also a really fun place to hang out at for both kids and adults because of all the interactive exhibits. If you're into science, you could spend an entire day here.

The National Museum of Emerging Science and Innovation. *katorisi*

• Museum of Maritime Science
Yu Fune-no-kagakukan; **R** Tokyo Teleport

Not far from the Miraikan, this museum can also make for a full-day experience with interactive displays all related to the ocean and observation rooms. The outside of the museum resembles a ship, so it's hard to miss.

The Museum of Maritime Science.

• Odaiba Seaside Park
Yu Odaiba-kaihinkoen; **R** Tokyo Teleport

You don't have to leave Tokyo to go to the beach. Although there's no swimming here, this is a place to sit in the sand at the water's edge, play beach volleyball or just enjoy the futuristic architecture.

While it might seem a little out of place, make sure you get a picture of the Statue of Liberty—donated to Japan by France to commemorate France Year. It's around 11 meters tall and weighs about nine tons.

• VenusFort
R Tokyo Teleport

There's a shopping mall right by the *Daikanransha* (p.118). The interior is decorated in the style of 17th or 18th century Europe, so you may even forget you're in Japan. It's indoors too, so you won't have to worry about rain.

• *Daikanransha* Ferris wheel
Yu Aomi; **R** Tokyo Teleport

At a height of 115 meters, this is one of the largest Ferris wheels in Japan, so it won't be hard to find. The ride is 16 minutes and offers you an incredible view of the surrounding area.

Get a great view of the area from 115 meters high.
Luis Villa del Campo

• Fuji TV Station
Yu Daiba; **R** Tokyo Teleport

This is the building with the huge ball at the top that serves as observatory deck. You can take an elevator up to the top, but you might have to stand in line. In addition, you can also

Fuji TV building with its observatory deck.
Mark J. Nelson and defchris

check out displays and buy merchandise for anime and TV shows broadcasted on the Fuji TV channel.

• Megaweb, Toyota City Showcase
Yu Aomi; **R** Tokyo Teleport

This place is more like a miniature amusement park than an automobile showcase. Don't miss the driving games and simulators, and the collection of old cars.

• Oedo-Onsen Monogatari
Yu Telecom Center; **R** Tokyo Teleport

This natural *onsen* (hot spring) theme park is the place to enjoy a variety of baths that take advantage of the water that gushes up from 1,400 meters underground. After or between bathing sessions, you can play games or go shopping wearing the *yukata* provided at the *onsen*. The entrance fee might be a little high, but you can easily spend four or five hours there.

Enjoy a hot bath *onsen* at Oasis in Tokyo.

If I were you, I would...

Go to Shinbashi Station on the Yamanote and before getting on the Yurikamome Line, think about getting a one-day pass. If you're a big walker, then you can walk to most of the sites in which case you should just buy one ticket from Shinbashi and one ticket back. Otherwise, the one-day pass is probably the way to go.

Then, choose one of the museums above depending on your tastes. That will keep you busy until around noon. After that, I'd head to Palette Town and go on the Ferris wheel. From there, you can head to VenusFort where you'll find lots of restaurants to choose from for lunch.

You then might want to go for a walk along the beach before heading to the Oedo-Onsen Monogatari hot springs. You'll probably also want to hang out at the *onsen* until the sun goes down, but try to make it back to the beach so you'll be able to see a beautiful sunset over the city—and maybe even catch a glimpse of the silhouetted Mt. Fuji. The best sunset views are probably from the beach, from the Ferris wheel or the Yurikamome train as it goes over Rainbow Bridge.

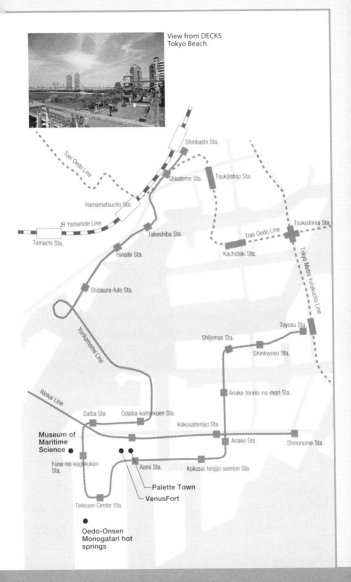

Musashino Area

Inokashira Park, Mount Takao, Jindaiji Temple, Jindaiji shopping street, Jindai Botanical Garden, Yumori-no-sato hot springs

Keywords:
- Temples
- Hot springs
- Botanical garden
- *Soba* noodles

This is one of my favorite places in Japan. Perhaps the best place to get away from it all for relaxation is Jindaiji. To get there, get on the Chuo Line and go to Kichijoji Station. Leaving from the Park Exit, go down the short escalator. Walk straight ahead out of the station up a narrow street to Marui Department Store. The bus stop is one of those in a line in front of the store (Bus 04 from Bus Stop 6), and then get off at Jindaiji (not Jindaiji Iriguchi)—or take a taxi. You'll find yourself in a pleasant little valley with hills on both sides.

• Inokashira Park
J K Kichijoji

This is one of Tokyo's best parks, and there's something especially impressive for every

Inokashira Park in western Tokyo is a great place to relax.

season. It's an ideal spot to enjoy the cherry blossoms or the changing leaves in autumn. The park also includes a zoo, beautiful temple and pond, and many walking courses.

The park is located south of Kichijoji Station, and to the north is one of the largest covered shopping areas in Tokyo. After visiting the park, it might be fun to take an hour or so to wander around to the other side of the station. The sun-roofed shopping arcade there has managed to retain both a regional and a trendy, stylish feel, making this a great day to spend a day—especially a rainy one!

• Mount Takao
J K Takao; K Takaosanguchi

If you came to Tokyo for the mountain hiking, then you have to go to Mt. Takao. Depending on your energy level, you can choose trails that call for climbing shoes, or paths that are more suited for regular street shoes.

It's an hour-and-a-half walk to the top, but you can just take the cable car or lift halfway up the mountain and walk the rest of the way if you'd rather not walk the whole way. The views of Tokyo and Mt. Fuji from the top of the mountain are amazing. If you're still not convinced, the 2007 edition of Michelin's Voyager Pratique Japon—the famous French travel guidebook—awarded Mt. Takao its maximum three stars.

• Jindaiji Temple
K Chofu; **J** Mitaka

This is the second oldest temple in Tokyo. Visitors are encouraged to walk around and explore the beautiful grounds where you might even get a chance to watch a ceremony of some type going on there. It's best to stand back and observe quietly and with respect.

If you want to avoid the touristy temples, this is the place to come.

• Jindaiji shopping street
K Chofu; **J** Mitaka

All of the shops around the temple have something traditional to offer—from traditional pastries and tea to *soba* noodles. This area is known for its *soba*. Although I don't think many people can distinguish these noodles from others anywhere in Japan, it won't be easy to find a nicer place to eat them.

• Jindai Botanical Garden
K Chofu; **J** Mitaka

At the top of the hill behind the temple, you'll find the entrance to the botanical gardens, and even if you're not that into plants, you'll still be impressed with this expansive and beautiful garden that has about 4,500 types of plants.

• Yumori-no-sato hot springs
K Chofu; **J** Musashi-sakai

If you walk over the hill opposite the Jindaiji Temple, you'll find the Yumori-no-sato *onsen* hot springs. It can be a little hard to find, but ask any stranger, and they'll probably be able to point you in the right direction. While its size isn't impressive, *onsen* lovers will thoroughly enjoy the the black mineral water.

If I were you, I would...

Try to get to Jindaiji in the morning by around 10:00. Then spend an hour or so exploring the shops and the temple, and after that, head to the botanical garden behind the temple. In front of the entrance are some of the loveliest restaurants you'll ever see, so you might want to stop for some *soba* before or after visiting the garden.

This is the place to enjoy beauty of trees, grass, and flowers in all seasons.

After seeing the garden, go for a leisurely walk for about 20 minutes to the hot springs. I could spend six or seven hours there, but maybe two or three is enough for most people. From the *onsen*, you can catch a free bus back to Musashisakai or Chofu station, from where you can head back to your hotel.

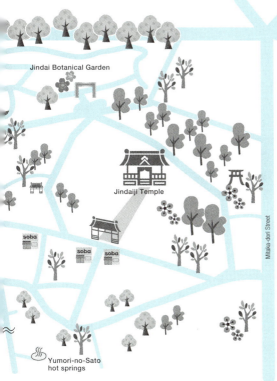

Kamakura Area

The Great Buddha Statue, Hase-dera Temple, Tsurugaoka Hachiman-gu, Tsurugaoka Hachiman-gu Treasury House, Komachi-dori, Other Kamakura temples, Enoshima, Shrines in Enoshima

Keywords:
- Temples and shrines
- History
- Beautiful nature and the ocean

Kamakura is a little like Kyoto and Nara, but much closer to Tokyo. While Tokyo has transformed mostly into a modern city, much of Kamakura has been preserved. It's located about an hour south of Tokyo by train. It's next to the ocean so it's famous for its sandy beaches.

If you're in a hurry, you can see most of the main spots in Kamakura in a day, but to really enjoy it at a relaxing pace, you might need two or three days.

The first thing you'll want to do when you arrive at the station is go to the Kamakura Tourist Information Service on the ground floor near the East Exit. They'll have lots of English maps and information to help you get oriented.

Kamakura is full of temples and shrines, many of which don't appear on the tourist maps. You might find that it's just as interesting to walk into a temple or shrine you find along the way as it is to see any site on the maps. So while a map will come in handy, let your heart be your guide. To get there, take the Shonan Shinjuku Line from Shinjuku station. Once you're at the station, you need to decide how you're going to get around.

• The Great Buddha Statue
E Hase

Located on the grounds of the Kotokuin Temple, *Daibutsu* (Buddha statue) is considered one of the main landmarks of Kamakura. The bronze statue is over 11 meters tall, with a width of 9.63 meters and a weight of 125 metric tons. The fact that it was built in the year 1252 makes it all the more amazing. More impressive than

The Great Buddha of Kamakura stands in Kotokuin Temple.

its size, though, is perhaps the statue's peaceful expression.

This *Daibutsu* was originally contained in a *Daibutsu* Hall, but the hall was destroyed long ago by a typhoon or tsunami, and the statue now sits exposed to the elements.

To get there by train, go to Hase Station on the Enoden Line that goes between Kamakura Station and Enoshima. From the station, it takes 10 to 15 minutes on foot. Just follow the road signs and the walking traffic.

• Hase-dera Temple
🇪 Hase

Stop here to see another huge wooden statue, one of the largest in Japan at 9.18 meters. The giant, gold-gilded *Juichimen Kannon* statue was carved, reportedly, from a huge camphor tree. The temple has a beautiful view of the bay. It's also famous for its hydrangeas flowers that bloom in June and July.

Hasedera Temple is famous for its hydrangeas blooming along the path in June and July.

• Tsurugaoka Hachiman-gu
🇯 🇪 Kamakura

Tsurugaoka Hachiman-gu is the main shrine in

Kamakura, and the main attraction. If you only have a few hours, then you'll probably want to just walk there (15 minutes) from the station. On the grounds, you'll find several sub-shrines and museums. The roots of the shrine date back to 1063. Possibly the most interesting things about the area are the architecture, ponds and beautiful nature.

For Japanese, there are two big times to visit the shrine. First, in the days after New Year's when about two million people visit the shrine to offer the first prayer of the year. It can take hours to get from the station to the shrine. The other busy time is when the cherry blossoms are in bloom in the spring. You'll want to plan your visit depending on how you feel about crowds.

After Minamoto no Yoritomo defeated a rival clan, he established the Kamakura Shogunate and became the first military leader in the Kamakura Period (1185-1333). He also

Tsurugaoka Hachiman-gu, founded in 1063, is the most important shrine in Kamakura.

made Kamakura his headquarters, making it the de facto capital of the nation. One of his first actions as Japan's new leader was to move the Hachiman-gu Shrine from Yuigahama to where it's located today.

Before the Meiji Restoration in 1868, Shintoism and Buddhism existed together on the grounds in harmony, but the Meiji government shook things up by making Shintoism the state religion and pushing Buddhism to the side. Many of the old buddhist buildings and statues were destroyed at that time.

- **Tsurugaoka Hachiman-gu Treasury House**
 🅹🅴 Kamakura

Located left of the main hall, the Treasure House is where you can see all the many valuable and historical objects such as swords, paintings, and statues dating back hundreds of years. If you know some Japanese history, the museum will be especially interesting.

- **Komachi-dori**
 🅹🅴 Kamakura

This is the shopping area located north of Kamakura Station on your way to Tsurugaoka

Hachiman-gu. It now has over 250 shops, cafes, restaurants and boutiques. You'll want to explore the many narrow alleys and discover some old Western-style houses, quaint shops and traditional treats.

• Other Kamakura temples

It would be very difficult to see all the temples and shrines of Kamakura, but if you enjoy this type of thing, then you will definitely want to see the following. There is often a small charge of 100 or 300 yen to enter the grounds.

○ Engaku-ji Temple

Founded in 1282, it is considered one of the most important Zen Buddhist temples, with its beautiful gardens and enormous cast-iron bell, which is a national treasure.

○ Tokei-ji Temple

Founded in 1285, it was originally a convent where men were forbidden to enter. It is also famous for its beautiful flowers.

○ Jochi-ji Temple

Founded in 1283, it is surrounded by cypress trees and bamboo groves with an unusual belfry at the main gate. Also interesting to see are the moss covered steps.

○ Meigetsu-in Temple

Founded in 1383, this temple is famous for its hydrangea flowers.

Meigetsu-in is a Rinzai Zen temple in Kita-Kamakura.

○ Kencho-ji Temple

Founded in 1253, this temple is very large and the oldest Zen training monastery in Japan. There is a dragon painting on the ceiling of the Ryuden Temple, one of its sub-temples, that is worth seeing.

Kencho-ji is the oldest Zen training monastery in Japan.

○ Zuisen-ji Temple

Founded in 1327, this temple provides a great view of Mt. Fuji, beautiful gardens with flowers and a pound, rock sculptures and a huge meditation cave.

The hall used for meditaion in Zuisen-ji Temple.

○ Hokoku-ji Temple

Founded in 1334, this temple is truly Zen with its relaxing bamboo forest that makes you feel like you need to whisper. Being there is like going to a theater and seeing an inspiring performance of light, sound and colors depending on the time of the year and the time of the day. The experience can be especially relaxing towards the end of a long day of sightseeing, but it closes at 4:00 p.m., so you'll want to get there by around 3:00 p.m.

○ Zeniarai-Benzaiten Ugafuku Shrine

It is said that Minamoto no Yoritomo was told to build this shrine in a dream. It has a gushing well where people believe that washing your money in the water will double its amount! It is also known for its symbolic *torii* gates and is surround by rock walls.

Zeniarai means "coin washing."
Σ64

○ Egara-tenjinsha Shrine

Founded in 1104, this shrine was dedicated to *Tenjin*, the god of education. Its bright red colors are magnificent.

- **Enoshima**

🅾 Katase-Enoshima; 🄴 Enoshima

This is a tiny little island connected to the mainland by a long bridge. There's a good chance that someone will be shooting a movie or TV show there whenever you go because it's such a scenic site.

Not far from the bridge to the island is the Enoshima Aquarium. There you can see a variety of interesting sea creatures.

Along the road of the entrance with a bronze shrine gate, there are a lot of quaint little shops. If you happen along a shop that sells one of Enoshima's specialties called *takosenbei*, an entire squire squashed flat and then baked, give it a try.

As you walk around, you'll notice the tower at the top of the island that has an incredible view of the ocean and Mt. Fuji on clear days.

View of Mt. Fuji from Enoshima.

There are some nice tea shops on the peak of the island. Try to find a place with a window seat for a wonderful view of the island and the surrounding area.

At the peak of the island, you can also find the Enoshima Samuel Cocking Garden, a small garden full of rare subtropical plants.

If you have enough time and energy, you might want to go down and see the caves and tidal pools, too.

• **Shrines in Enoshima**

The Shinto shrines scattered around the island are collectively known as Enoshima Shrine, and they are dedicated to *Benten*, a popular goddess of luck, wealth, music and knowledge. The myth is that *Benten* created the small island before killing a five headed dragon that had been terrorizing the area.

One of the many Shinto shrines on Enoshima.

If I were you, I would...

Leave early and rent a bicycle from the shop located at the east exit of Kamakura Station. They'll give you a map (English available), that will help you to get around to all the sites. If you can, pay a little extra for an electric bicycle. There are a lot of hills and inclines in Kamakura, so it'll make all the difference. Head south to Enoshima, and after crossing the bridge to the island, park your bike and walk around.

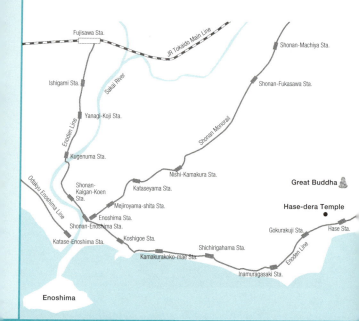

Then, head back to Kamakura, but when you get to Hase Station, turn left and go to the Great Buddha. Keep going north towards Kita-Kamakura Station. Visit the following temples and shrines in this order: Hase-dera Temple, Zeniarai-Benzaiten Ugafuku Shrine, Jochi-ji Temple, Tokei-ji Temple, Engaku-ji Temple, Meigetsu-in Temple and Kencho-ji Temple. There are a lot of temples, so you may want to skip some of them. Then go to Tsurugaoka Hachiman-gu.

If after all of that, if you still want to see Hokoku-ji Temple and its bamboo forest, then head east. After that, head back to Tsurugaoka Hachiman-gu. Then, push your bicycle through the crowded Komachi-dori Street as you head back to the station. Those with more time and energy can head to Yuigahama Beach, where they'll hopefully be in time to catch a beautiful sunset.

Appendix

Everything else

Watch and Play

• Tokyo Disneyland and Disney Sea
Y Maihama; **S** Urayasu

This is the main destination for a lot of visitors to Japan, although there's nothing particularly Japanese here. If the weather is nice, then the lines are going to be long, so I would try to go on a cloudy day.

• Sumo wrestling
JS Ryogoku

The Kokugikan in Ryogoku is the place to go. It hosts three of the six annual sumo tournaments in January, May and September. Ask your hotel or check the Internet for tickets. Even if you aren't in Tokyo during those months, you can still walk around the area and enjoy the sumo-related attractions. The *chanko-nabe* restaurants that serve dishes typically eaten by training sumo wrestlers are great for culture enthusiasts, but not for the light eater.

This dish contains chicken, fish, *tofu*, vegetables and whatever happens to be available.

• Edo Tokyo museum
🟦J🟦S Ryogoku

If you go to the Kokugikan in Ryogoku to exerience sumo, you'll probably also want to take in the Edo-Tokyo Museum. You probably won't spend more than an hour here, but it is a good place to get a feel for what Tokyo was like 100 years ago.

• Tokyo Wild Bird Park
🟦M Ryutsu Center

Surprisingly close to the center of Tokyo, this enormous park has several lakes, thick brush and wooded areas, marshes and even mudflats. But it's not exactly quiet; heavy traffic is all around and there are even airplanes flying above, but it doesn't seem to bother all the various types of birds you're likely to see.

Give it a Try

• Capsule hotels

I'm sure you've heard about these hotels that are actually capsules you can sleep in to save money in crowded Tokyo. They are popular for their comfort and convenience. Most of the major train stations will have at least one capsule hotel nearby for non-claustrophobic travelers.

• Bus tours

One of the least complicated ways to see Tokyo and the surrounding areas is on a one-day bus tour, and Hato Bus (http://www.hatobus.com/en/) is the main provider. Their English tours start from around 4,500 yen for a half day, while full-day tours can exceed 10,000 yen. It's an easy and friendly experience, providing a very productive day of sightseeing.

• Cat cafes

A lot of apartments in Tokyo don't allow pets, so cat cafes have sprung up all over the city. Your hotel can probably help you find one nearby, or you might see one while wandering around. For not much more than the price of a cup of coffee, you'll be able to cuddle with a kitten.

- **Become a ninja**

Do a search for "Ninja Spy Action Workshop" and you'll find an organization that provides some pretty serious ninja training. The workshops start at 18,000 yen for 60 to 80 minutes, but it seems like most participates have a great experience.

- **Zen meditation**
🇯 🇸 Ueno

Several temples in Japan offer meditation sessions open to the public and English speakers. I recommend the Tokuun-in temple, a five-minute walk from Ueno Station, on the other side of the park. Sessions include *zazen* meditation, chanting and tea ceremony. The sessions are on Fridays from 7:00 a.m. to 9:15 a.m., but you'll need to arrive at 6:30 a.m. for first-time orientation. E-mail your intention to participate to tokyozazen@jcom.home.ne.jp.

Places to Visit

• Sugamo
Y S Sugamo

Sugamo Jizo-dori Shopping Street.

This is where the silver generation can have a good time. A shopping area north of the station is crowded with little shops offering all kinds of goods, old-fashioned street food, health teas, and even the popular health-inducing red underpants. It's a great way to spend a couple of leisurely hours.

• Yanaka
J Nippori

The shopping district on the west side of the Nippori Station is filled with rustic charm and small shops selling a variety of cute things. It's a wonderful place to spend an easy afternoon. If you really want to get away from Tokyo's chaos, walk through the nearby Yanaka cemetery.

A large cemetery north of Ueno, famous for its beautiful cherry blossoms.

Everything else 147

• Roppongi
S Roppongi

Party animals probably already know about Roppongi. It's the place to go for dancing and drinking, and since it's a gathering spot for foreigners, everyone is generally tolerant of a certain degree of rowdiness.

• Tokyo Midtown
S Roppongi, Nogizaka, Roppongi-itchome

If you're tired of staying at backpacker hotels, then spend a few nights at the Ritz Carlton, located in the huge Tokyo Midtown commercial complex. It's also the place to go for high-end shopping and dining in the Roppongi area.

Opened in 2007, the Tokyo Midtown complex has offices, shops, restaurants, museums, apartments, and a hotel.

Holidays in Japan

- **January 1, New Year's Day (*ganjitsu*)**
  official holiday
  Only January 1 is designated as a national holiday, but most businesses remain closed through January 3.

- **Second Monday of January, Coming of Age (*seijin no hi*)** *official holiday*
  The coming of age of 20 year olds is celebrated on this national holiday.

- **February 3, Beginning of spring (*setsubun*)**
  This is not a national holiday, but celebrated at shrines and temples nationwide.

- **February 11, National Foundation Day (*kenkoku kinen no hi*)** *official holiday*
  According to the earliest Japanese history records, on this day in the year 660 BC the first Japanese emperor was crowned.

- **February 14, Valentine's Day**
  In Japan, women give chocolates to men on Valentine's Day.

- **March 3, Doll's Festival (*hina matsuri*)**
  Also called girl's festival.

- March 14, White Day

  The opposite of Valentine's Day: Men give white chocolates to women.

- Around March 20, Spring Equinox Day *(shunbun no hi)* *official holiday*

  Graves are visited during the week *(ohigan)* of the Equinox Day.

- April 29, Showa Day *(Showa no hi)* *official holiday*

  The birthday of former Emperor Showa. Before 2007, April 29 was known as Greenery Day (now celebrated on May 4). Showa Day is part of the Golden Week.

- May 3, Constitution Day *(kenpo kinenbi)* *official holiday*

  A national holiday remembering the new constitution, which was put into effect after the war.

- May 4, Greenery Day *(midori no hi)* *official holiday*

  Until 2006, Greenery Day was celebrated on April 29, the former Emperor Showa's birthday, due to the emperor's love for plants and nature. It is now celebrated on May 4 and is part of the Golden Week.

- May 5, Children's Day *(kodomo no hi)* *official holiday*

Also called boy's festival.

- **July/August 7, Star Festival (*tanabata*)**
  Tanabata is a festival rather than a national holiday.

- **Third Monday of July, Ocean Day (*umi no hi*)** *official holiday*
  A recently introduced national holiday to celebrate the ocean. The day marks the return of Emperor Meiji from a boat trip to Hokkaido in 1876.

- **August 11, Mountain Day (*yama no hi*)**
  national holiday from 2016
  This national holiday will be newly introduced from the year 2016 to celebrate mountains.

- **July/August 13-15, *Obon***
  Obon is a festival to commemorate deceased ancestors.

- **Third Monday of September, Respect for the Aged Day (*keiro no hi*)** *official holiday*
  Respect for the elderly and longevity are celebrated on this national holiday.

- **Around September 23, Autum Equinox Day (*shubun no hi*)** *official holiday*
  Graves are visited during the week (*ohigan*) of the Equinox Day.

- **Second Monday of October, Health and Sports Day (*taiiku no hi*)** *official holiday*
  On that day in 1964, the Olympic games of Tokyo were opened.

- **November 3, Culture Day (*bunka no hi*)** *official holiday*
  A day for promotion of culture and the love of freedom and peace. On culture day, schools and the government award selected persons for their special, cultural achievements.

- **November 15, Seven-Five-Three (*shichigosan*)**
  A festival for children, *Shichigosan* is not a national holiday.

- **November 23, Labour Thanksgiving Day (*kinro kansha no hi*)** *official holiday*
  A national holiday for honoring labour.

- **December 23, Emperor's Birthday (*tenno tanjobi*)** *official holiday*
  The birthday of the current emperor is always a national holiday. If the emperor changes, the national holiday changes to the birthday date of the new emperor.

- **December 31, New Year's Eve (*omisoka*)**
  December 31 is not a national holiday, but most businesses are closed.

Who to call

- Tokyo English-speaking Police: 03-3501-0110 (weekdays 8:30 a.m. to 5:15 p.m.)
- Tokyo Emergency First Aid Association: 03-5276-0995
- Tokyo Metropolitan Medical Institution Information Service provides a telephone-emergency translation service: 03-5285-8185
- Japan Help Line, 24-hour worldwide emergency assistance with English-speaking volunteer operators: 05-7000-0911
- Tourist Information Center: 03-3201-3331 (9:00 a.m. to 5:00 p.m. on weekdays, 9:00 a.m. to 12:00 noon on Saturdays)
- Police: 110 (English-speaking operator available 24-hours)
- Fire: 119 (English-speaking operator available 24-hours)
- Ambulance: 119 (English-speaking operator available 24-hours)
- Phone Directory: 104 (English-speaking operator available 9:00 a.m. to 8:00 p.m.)
- Tokyo Fire Dept.: 03-3212-2323 (information service, such as hospital info, available 24-hours)
- Tokyo English Life Line: 03-5774-0992 (Available daily 9:00 a.m. to 11:00 p.m.)

Index

A

Akasaka Hikawa Shrine.... *111*
Akihabara Electronics City
....*82*
Ameyoko *65, 82, 84*
Aqua City Odaiba *115*
Asakusa Samba Carnival.... *61*

B

bed-and-breakfast *18*
beer gardens *63*
bento......................................*14*
bicycle rental shoop *13*
bicycles *13*
bills..*37*
bowing *30*
breakfast *23*
Bridgestone Museum of Art
....*92*
bus tours........................*11, 145*
buses.....................................*11*
business card *30*
business hotel *18*

C

capsule hotel *18*
cash..*37*
cherry blossoms *55*
Chidorigafuchi Koen............*55*
Christmas *48*
Christmas lights...................*51*
coins.....................................*37*
Comiket *63*
Coming of Age Day

D

ceremonies........................*49*
converting money................*36*
credit cards *37*

Daikanransha Ferris wheel
.... *118*
debit cards............................*37*
delicatessen/food floor........*40*
dinner *25*

E

earthquake *44*
East Garden (of the Imperial
   Palace) *58, 88, 94*
Eastern Shinjuku *103*
Echigo Yuzawa......................*50*
Engaku-ji Temple *133*
Enoshima..............................*136*
Enoshima Aquarium *136*
Enoshima Samuel Cocking
   Garden *137*
Enoshima Shrine *137*

F

flea market *56*
Fuji TV Station..................... *118*
Fujifilm Square................... *110*

G

gay bars *104*
General Nogi's Residence
.... *110*
genkan...................................*31*
gingko (nuts) *67*

154

Ginza 89
Golden Gai 104
Great Buddha Statue, the .. 129

H

Hachiko Exit 97
Hama Rikyu Garden 68
Hanazono Shrine 104
Harajuku 99
Harajuku-Omotesando Hello Halloween Pumpkin Parade 66
Hase-dera Temple 130
Hato Bus tour 12, 145
Hibiya park 57
Higashi Gyoen 88
high-end hotels 16
high-end inns 16
Hokoku-ji Temple 134
hot pot 49
hot springs 33, 50
hotels 16, 18, 20

i

Imperial Palace, the 88
Inokashira Park 68, 122

J

Jindai Botanical Garden 125
Jindaiji shopping street 125
Jindaiji Temple 124
Jochi-ji Temple 133
Juichimen Kannon statue 130

K

Kabukicho 103
Kabuki-za Theater, the 90
kaiten-zushi restaurant 25
Kappabashi Dogu Street 76
Karuizawa 50
Kencho-ji Temple 134
kissaten 23
koban 42
Koishikawa Korakuen 52
Komachi-dori 132
Korean town, Little 105
Kotokuin Temple 129
kumade 47
Kurayami Festival 54
Kyu Shiba Rikyu Garden 68

L

local buses 11
lost 42
low-end hotels 18
low-end inns 18
lunch 24
lunch-boxes 14

M

maid cafe 83
mamachari 13
medical care 43
Megaweb, Toyota City Showcase 119
Meigetsu-in Temple 134
Meiji Shrine 99
menus 22
Metropolitan buses 11
minshuku 18
Miraikan 116
Mitsukoshi Department Store 92
money 36

Index 155

Mori Art Museum............... *108*
Mori Arts Center Gallery... *108*
morning service............. *21, 23*
morning set........................*23*
museum...............................*69*
Museum of Maritime Science *116*

N

nabe......................................*49*
National Art Center, the.... *110*
National Museum of Emerging Science and Innovation, the *71, 116*
New Year's holiday..............*48*
Nezu Shrine.........................*81*
Nihonbashi........................ *191*
Nogi Shrine......................... *110*

O

Odaiba Cinema Mediage... *115*
Odaiba Seaside Park *117*
Odaiba's Aqua City............ *115*
Oedo-Onsen Monogatari *50, 119*
okonomiyaki........................*26*
Omoide-yokocho *102*
Omotesando *51, 99*
Omotesando Hills.............. *101*
100-yen stores *39*
onsen *33, 50*
Otemachi.............................*87*
outdoor performances *57*

P

Panasonic Center............... *115*
police *42*
police boxes *42*
price......................................*23*
public gardens......................*67*

R

Rainbow Bridge *115*
Ramen Kokugikan theme park *115*
rental bicycle.......................*13*
Rikugien *68*
Ritz Carlton Hotel...... *109, 148*
river ferry *70*
Roppongi Hills.................... *108*
Roppongi Hills Arena *109*
rush hour...............................*9*
ryokan *16*

S

Sanja Festival *55*
Saury Festival in Meguro....*66*
seiza *34*
Senso-ji Temple................... *76*
Shibuya................................ *96*
Shibuya Scramble Crossing *97*
SHIBUYA109........................*97*
Shinjuku Eisa Festival *61*
Shinjuku Gyoen............ *68, 104*
Shinobazunoike pond *61*
Shin-Okubo *105*
shitamachi............................ *75*
Shitamachi Museum...... *64, 84*
Shomben-yokocho............. *102*
shopping...............................*36*
sick..*43*
skiing *50*
Southern Shinjuku............. *105*
Spa LaQua *50, 53*
Star Festival *62, 151*
Statue of Liberty................ *117*

street food 26
street vendors 26
subculture 63
Sumida River Fireworks Festival 62
Suntory Museum of Art 110

T

Takao, Mt. 56, 123
Takashimaya Times Square 105
Takeshita Street 99
Taking off your shoes 31
takoyaki 26
Tanabata Festival 62, 151
Taro Okamoto MemoriaMuseum 69
tatami 16, 31
taxis 10
TENQ 53
tipping 23
Togo Shrine 100
TOHO Cinemas Roppongi Hills 109
Tokei-ji Temple 133
Tokyo Dome 50
Tokyo Metropolitan Art Museum 84
Tokyo Midtown 109, 148
Tokyo Sea Life Park 70
Tokyo Skytree 77
Tokyo Station Building 86
Tori-no-ichi festival 47
trains 9, 32
Tsukiji Fish Market 92
Tsuruoka Hachiman-gu 130
Tsuruoka Hachiman-gu Treasury House 132

tuna auction 93
2-chome gay district 104
2k540 AKI-OKA ARTISAN 84

U

Ueno Onshi Park 55, 57, 66, 69, 82
Ueno Summer Festival 61

V

vegetarians 27
VenusFort 117
visiting someone's home 31

W

wake-up call 20
Western Shinjuku 102
Women only train cars 15

Y

yakitori 25, 26
yakitori restaurant 25
Yanaka Ginza shopping street 81
Yanesen 80
Yasukuni Shrine 58
youth hostels 18
Yoyogi park 56, 57, 98
yukata 20
Yumori-no-sato hot springs 125

Z

Zeniarai-Benzaiten Ugafuku Shrine 135
Zuisen-ji Temple 134

Index 157

photo David Thayne (p.76 bottom, p.84, p.101, p.147),
　　　 photolibrary, Wikipedia

Map　結城　麗, IBC Publishing

TOKYO CITY GUIDE

2015年5月9日　第1刷発行

著　者　　デイビッド・セイン

発行者　　浦　　晋 亮

発行所　　**IBCパブリッシング株式会社**
　　　　　〒162-0804 東京都新宿区中里町29番3号 菱秀神楽坂ビル 9F
　　　　　Tel. 03-3513-4511　Fax. 03-3513-4512
　　　　　www.ibcpub.co.jp

印刷所　　株式会社シナノパブリッシングプレス

© A to Z 2014
© IBC パブリッシング 2014
Printed in Japan

落丁本・乱丁本は、小社宛にお送りください。送料小社負担にてお取り替えいたします。
本書の無断複写 (コピー) は著作権法上での例外を除き禁じられています。

ISBN978-4-7946-0345-6

SHINJUKU / SHIBUYA / ROPPONGI AREA

To Ikebukuro/Ueno

Shin-Okubo Sta.

To Nakano

Shinjuku Sta.

Shinjuku p. 102

Shinjuku-gyoemmae Sta.

Tokyo Metro Marunouchi Line

To Tokyo/Chi...

To Ogikubo

Shinjuku Gyoen National Garden p.68, 104

Yotsuya Sta.

To Gin.../Tokyo

Meiji Shrine p.99, 100

Sendagaya Sta.

Chuo-Sobu Line

Shinanomachi Sta.

Harajuku Sta.

Yoyogi Park p.56, 57, 98

Harajuku p.99

Shibuya p.96

Shibuya Sta.

Tokyo Midtown p.109, 148

To Akihab.../Ueno

Yamanote Line

Roppongi Sta.

Ebisu Sta.

Tokyo Metro Hibiya Line

To Nakameguro/Yokohama

To Meguro/Shinagawa

Map locations are not accurate to scale.

ASAKUSA / UENO / TOKYO AREA

- Nippori-Toneri Liner
- Nippori Sta.
- Uguisudani Sta.
- Yanaka p.80
- Ueno Sta.
- Asakusa p.61, 75
- Ueno Zoological Gardens p.82, 84
- Ueno Onshi Park p.55, 57, 66, 69, 82
- Okachimachi Sta.
- Ameyoko Shopping Street p.65, 82, 84
- Tokyo Skytree p.77
- Ochanomizu Sta.
- Akihabara Sta.
- Sobu Main Line
- Chuo Line
- Akihabara p.82
- Kanda Sta.
- Tokyo Sta. p.86
- Tokyo Sta.
- Yamanote Line
- Imperial Palace p.58, 88, 94
- Tsukiji Fish Market p.92
- Yurakucho Sta.

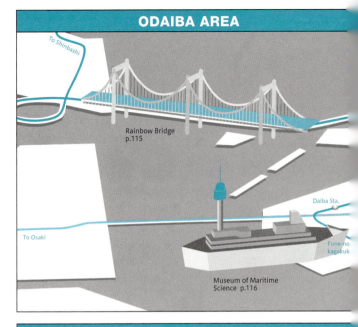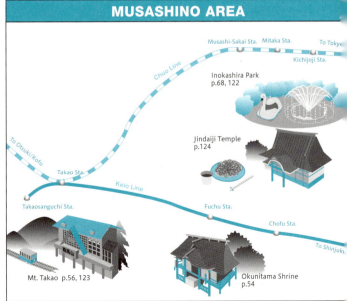